When God Whispers

# When God Whispers

Glimpses of an
Extraordinary God
By an
Ordinary Woman

Carole Mayhall

**NAVPRESS**
BRINGING TRUTH TO LIFE
NavPress Publishing Group
P.O. Box 35001, Colorado Springs, Colorado 80935

The Navigators is an international Christian organization. Jesus Christ gave His followers the Great Commission to go and make disciples (Matthew 28:19). The aim of The Navigators is to help fulfill that commission by multiplying laborers for Christ in every nation.

NavPress is the publishing ministry of The Navigators. NavPress publications are tools to help Christians grow. Although publications alone cannot make disciples or change lives, they can help believers learn biblical discipleship, and apply what they learn to their lives and ministries.

Library of Congress Catalog Card Number:
    93-48513
ISBN 08910-97716

Cover illustration: Marcia Smith

Some of the anecdotal illustrations in this book are true to life and are included with the permission of the persons involved. All other illustrations are composites of real situations, and any resemblance to people living or dead is coincidental.

Unless otherwise identified, all Scripture quotations in this publication are taken from the *HOLY BIBLE: NEW INTERNA-TIONAL VERSION*® (NIV®). Copyright ©1973, 1978, 1984 by International Bible Society. Used by permission of Zondervan Publishing House. All rights reserved. Other versions used include: the *New American Standard Bible* (NASB), © The Lockman Foundation 1960, 1962, 1963, 1968, 1971, 1972, 1973, 1975, 1977; *The New Testament in Modern English* (PH), J.B. Phillips Translator, © J.B. Phillips 1958, 1960, 1972, used by per-mission of Macmillan Publishing Company; *The Living Bible* (TLB), © 1971, used by permission of Tyndale House Publishers, 60189, all rights reserved; and the *King James Version* (KJV).

Mayhall, Carole.
    When God whispers : glimpses of an extraordinary God by an ordinary woman / Carole Mayhall.
        p. cm.
    ISBN 0-89109-771-6
    1. Christian life—1960- 2. Women—Prayer-books and devotions—English. 3. Mayhall, Carole. I. Title.
BV4501.2.M4255  1994
242'.643—dc20                                          93-48513
                                                            CIP

Printed in the United States of America

FOR A FREE CATALOG OF
NAVPRESS BOOKS & BIBLE STUDIES,
CALL 1-800-366-7788 (USA)
or 1-416-499-4615 (CANADA)

# Contents

*To special friends
who . . . over the years . . .
in innumerable ways . . .
have gone before me or have come alongside me —
to help this very ordinary woman continue to glimpse
an extraordinary God*

# Introduction

$\mathcal{I}$ think there are a lot of people in the world like me.

People who often are rushing on the outside.

Rushing on the inside too.

People who long for inside quietness and peace.

People who are feeling frazzled, frantic, frustrated.

People who wonder where the joy went, who feel useless, needy, ordinary.

But people who also long to hear God through those very weary, sometimes empty moments.

I think . . . for most of us, most of the time . . . God doesn't manifest Himself in spectacular revelations. Instead, He shows Himself to us in the slightly out-of-the-ordinary moments that appear, not as giant crashing waves, but as gentle ripples lapping onto the beaches of life.

We mortals rarely see God's astonishing cloud and fire settling on a holy mountain. Instead we see Him in the daily routines of work and play and meditation.

Few of us have known the wonder that Moses felt standing at the burning bush or have seen God's awesome glory pass by us as He hides us in a cleft of a rock.

But, if we have looked for Him, we *have* seen Him! We have heard the still, small voice of His Spirit in our hearts; we have felt His presence in a hundred special moments; we have watched Him work in times of ecstasy, grief, joy, pain, love, mourning, despair, hope, and in the humdrum of the daily moments of life.

For me, God has revealed Himself mostly in glimpses. Looking back on my life, I remember a few startling revelations, but usually I have seen Him . . . and learned His lessons . . . in the context of everyday events.

That's what this book is about: everyday events. God speaking in the ordinary, the mundane, the commonplace, the average, the routine of daily life.

It's a book about the whispers of God. Whispers of love to an ordinary woman . . . beholding an extraordinary God!

These are some of the important people in my life who are a part of my glimpses:

Jack — my husband
Lynn — our daughter
Tim — our son-in-law
Eric — our grandson
Sonya Marie or "Sunny" — our granddaughter

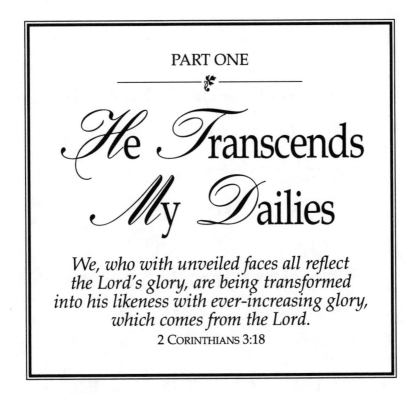

# PART ONE

## He Transcends My Dailies

*We, who with unveiled faces all reflect the Lord's glory, are being transformed into his likeness with ever-increasing glory, which comes from the Lord.*

2 CORINTHIANS 3:18

———— ❧ ————

*M*OST OF US HATE THE WORD *ORDINARY*. WE DESPISE THE WORD *AVERAGE*. WE DETEST THE MUNDANE AND COMMONPLACE.

BUT THAT'S WHERE I LIVE. AND THAT'S WHO I AM.

UNTIL I SEE GOD IN THE "DAILIES," I DESPAIR. BUT AS I SEE HIM IN THE ORDINARY, COMMON THINGS, I ATTEST TO THE TRUTH THAT THERE IS *GLORY* IN THE ORDINARY, BECAUSE OF . . . JESUS!

# ONE

# Ordinary Is Okay

felt especially frumpy that morning after traveling in the car for three days through snow and rain, sleeping in a different bed each night. War news had sobered and distracted us. Yet I needed to be focused, to be "up," to be ready for the weekend conference.

In the car that morning, I read in Ephesians, "We are God's workmanship."

Glancing down at my dirty sweater and spotty slacks, I ran a hand through my messy hair and thought, *Kind of sloppy work, Lord!* Mentally a hand flew to my mouth in denial of that disrespectful thought.

"You are My workmanship," a voice repeated in my mind. "*I have never made anything imperfect.*"

"Your hand didn't slip when You made me, Lord?" I questioned silently.

"No, child," I heard Him answer.

"You didn't get distracted and forget what You were doing?"

"No, beloved."

"Then *this* (I glanced in the car mirror) . . . this is deliberate?"

"Yes, daughter, it is. If you read on, I'll explain."

"Created in Christ Jesus to do good works which God prepared in advance for us to do."

Ah.

"Let's see if I'm getting this, Lord. This rather lumpy clay pot is shaped and constructed for maximum effectiveness for the *specific* good works You planned ahead of time for me personally. Is that right, Lord?"

"That's correct, dear one."

"But . . ." I began.

"Carole, let's get this settled." He spoke firmly to my heart. "If I'd made you physically beautiful, you'd be admired. If I'd made you with showy talent, you'd be held in awe. If I'd birthed you to a wealthy family, you'd be envied. If I'd given you exceptional intellect, you'd be relegated to ivory towers.

"Instead, Carole, I made you a bit lumpy, gave you an unexceptional face, commonplace capabilities, unremarkable talents. You see, for the good works I prepared in advance for *you* to do, I needed an average, ordinary woman to identify with a great many others just like you."

I wondered then how many women traveling toward that conference had spotty slacks and messy hair. . . . Well, I had news for *them*!

I whispered, "Lord, are You saying it's okay to be ordinary?"

My Father answered, "Dear one, ordinary is not in My vocabulary. To Me, each child is extraordinary—including *you!*"

---

*Lord, thank You for creating me so carefully and uniquely. Help me to celebrate Your workmanship by offering all of who I am to Your world today.*

We are God's workmanship, created in Christ Jesus to do good works, which God prepared in advance for us to do. (Ephesians 2:10)

# TWO

# *Meadowlarks*

t was a pristine, state-of-the-art spring day in Washington state — snow-capped mountains, sparkling bays, brilliant flowers. Driving along a picturesque country road, we passed a well-groomed farm with a trim rail fence and saw a neatly lettered sign that said:

PLEASE DRIVE QUIETLY

Some music notes followed the letters. We puzzled over the meaning until we spied another sign fifty yards further. Trailed by more music notes, it read:

MEDOWLARKS SINGING

I had a great urge to yell at Jack, "*Pull off the road. Stop the car! Turn off the engine!*" so we could sit and hear the stillness — and the meadowlarks singing!

There are times in my life when I need to pull off to the side of the road, stop the clamoring engine of the world around me, and *listen*. Listen to God. . . . And listen to His meadowlarks singing.

But I'm usually going too fast to listen. I'm too busy to stop. Rushing too headlong to hear.

This morning I read the words of a familiar psalm — a psalm that fairly breathes quietness:

The LORD is my shepherd, I shall not be in want.
    He makes me lie down in green pastures,
he leads me beside quiet waters,
    he restores my soul. (Psalm 23:1-3)

In the bustle of brimming-full days, when I hear only strident voices and roaring engines, God's meadowlarks keep singing. But how can my heart be cheered, or my soul be stirred, or my spirit be lifted in joy, when I don't *hear*? How can He lead me beside the still waters when I've kicked into passing gear in the fast lane of life? How can God *restore my soul* when I don't take time to sit at the feet of Jesus?

*Father God, in my everyday busyness, in the bustle and hustle of my days, in the clamor of the world around me, remind me to take frequent moments to pull off the road, stop the car, turn off the engine, and listen to You and to Your meadowlarks . . . singing.*

Let the morning bring me word of your unfailing love,
    for I have put my trust in you.
Show me the way I should go,
    for to you I lift up my soul. (Psalm 143:8)

# THREE

# *Business Cards*

———◦———

"*D*o you have a business card?"

The question came abruptly from a tailored, well-manicured woman, and I flushed.

"No, I don't, but I'll write out my address for you if you have something to write on," I responded, chagrined that I didn't have a pad of paper in my bulging purse.

*Caught again*, I thought. *Does* everybody *have business cards these days? Everybody except me?*

My mind began to percolate.

"Let's see," I said to myself, "what would I put on a business card?"

On a day when I played golf with friend-husband, it could state:

Carole Mayhall, Terrible Golfer

On a day when I busied myself in matters around the house, I'd write:

Carole Mayhall, Busy Homemaker

On another day spent at my computer, I'd use:

Carole Mayhall, Sometimes Writer, degree in letters

Yeah, I like that! — but would anyone else get it?

Then I got carried away. How about Contented Wife (no, that sounds too much like a contented cow). Perhaps Happy Wife (no, that's too close to Happy Valley Salad Dressing).

I know, Loving Wife and Mother. *Yuk.* That's for a tombstone.

Oh, well.

Perhaps I should go with Shakespeare:

Carole Mayhall, Much Ado About Nothing

I realized this exercise could go on and on and leave me more frustrated and embarrassed than before. So finally I came to the conclusion that, should I ever decide to have a business card printed, I would like it simply to read:

Carole Mayhall, Child of God

*Father, though my life is woven together with many complex roles and responsibilities — serious and otherwise — help me to keep in my heart the wonder of being, above all, Your child.*

> Consider what he has done — before the foundation of
> the world he chose us to become, in Christ, his holy
> and blameless children living within his constant care.
> He planned, in his purpose of love, that we should be
> adopted as his own children through Jesus Christ. . . .
> And here is the staggering thing — that in all which
> will one day belong to him we have been promised a
> share. (Ephesians 1:4-5,10; PH)

FOUR
# *Feeling Inadequate*

*E*very women's church retreat has to have a fun night, and this one was amazing. Skits. Songs. Craziness. Then to top it off, a stylish woman demonstrated the best colors for each "season," makeup, new fashions. I took it all in.

Sunday morning I got up and began my routine. I looked in the mirror and told myself, "You know, I'm putting my makeup on all wrong! I should be smoothing *away* from my eyes and more toward the center. And oh, yes, my foundation should be lighter than my skin tone."

I began to put on my red suit and thought, "This is *just* the right length—for four years ago! And it is *just* the right color—for someone else's season." (I confess, I knew that when I bought it—the red needs more yellow tone in it, but I liked it enough to buy it anyway.)

My thoughts continued, "Oh dear, I'm tying this scarf all wrong—this year it's 'simple' not 'cute,' so the lady says. But at least I have on only nine articles of whatever—I think! Let's see, glasses count one, a watch that 'makes a statement' counts one—but mine doesn't, so it doesn't count. . . . I *have* left my jacket open, which is the 'power' way to do it! So I'm doing *something* right. . . . Right?"

I looked at myself again in the mirror and felt all wrong. Insecure. Inadequate.

Then I started to laugh as Bible verses started to tug at the corners of my mind. I thought of the psalm that says, "You

19

are a shield around me, O LORD; you bestow glory on me and lift up my head" (3:3); and "He brought me out into a spacious place; he rescued me because he delighted in me" (18:19). If God Himself bestows glory on me and delights in me, then what does it matter if I tie my scarf wrong for this season?

And He "lifts up my head." In my imagination, I saw myself, head drooping in discouragement, and the Lord gently putting His hand under my chin, lifting my face toward Himself, and saying, "Cheer up, beloved child."

It's a lesson I need to be reminded of often. Years ago I listened to a woman speak about self-worth and how most of us base our self-worth on how we perceive *other* people perceive us. Others judge us, or so we're convinced, on the three-legged stool of our appearance, our performance, and our status. Because all of us are lacking in at least one of those qualities, the stool collapses and our self-worth with it.

This same speaker said that instead of looking into the mirror of other people's opinions about us, we constantly need to look into the mirror of God's love for us — a love that is unconditional, accepting, extraordinary. If I look into that mirror, instead of being worried about my "self-worth," I'll have "God-worth," which is *so much better*.

I'd listened, realized the truth of what she said, and tried to practice it day by day. But . . . one more time . . . I'd forgotten.

"Lord, I'm doing it again!" I confessed. "How many times have You told me that my security and adequacy can be only in *You*. Not in how I'm dressed. Not in how I look. Not in how I perform. Not in how I'm accepted. But in *You*."

I need to hang on to that precious thought constantly.

But especially after listening to a fashion expert!

*Father, my focus gets fuzzy so quickly. Teach me to know in my heart, as well as in my head, that my security isn't in how I look or in what I do well, but only in You and in Your love.*

Long ago, even before he made the world, God chose us
to be his very own, through what Christ would do for
us; he decided then to make us holy in his eyes, without
a single fault—we who stand before him covered with
his love. His unchanging plan has always been to adopt
us into his own family by sending Jesus Christ to die for
us. And he did this because he wanted to!

Now all praise to God for his wonderful kindness
to us and his favor that he has poured out upon us,
because we belong to his dearly loved Son. So overflowing is his kindness towards us that he took away
all our sins through the blood of his Son, by whom we
are saved; and he has showered down upon us the
richness of his grace—for how well he understands us
and knows what is best for us at all times. . . .

Moreover, because of what Christ has done we
have become gifts to God *that he delights in*. (Ephesians
1:4-8,11; TLB; emphasis added)

# FIVE

# Boredom

He snow blew in after us, as my friend and I walked into the quaint restaurant. We were shown to a table near a roaring fire in a great stone fireplace.

Over coffee, I asked casually, "How are things with you? What's happening in your life these days?"

She made a flat motion with her hand and responded, "Nothing. Absolutely nothing." She shrugged her shoulders in a gesture of hopelessness.

*Strange*, I thought as I looked at this attractive widow, full of vitality. Her beautifully cut, prematurely gray hair framed her youthful face. She had told me that she was into a lot of things . . . seminar speaking, leading a Bible study, finishing a course in real estate.

She wondered about the dullness. She had gone through periods of apathy since her husband had died a few years before. The "zip" in her life was gone; she couldn't see herself being used by God in a way that she wanted to be or that was fulfilling to her. During certain periods she had questioned if the Lord really cared about her.

She was the second woman that week who had said similar words and expressed that life was, in a word, *boring*.

Boredom can rob a person of *joy*. Apathy may not sink my boat, but it can becalm me and cause despair as the wind is taken out of the sails of my life.

I cupped my hands around the mug of hot coffee before

me and thought about two verses in Proverbs (8:30-31). Wisdom (Christ) is speaking, "I was filled with delight day after day, rejoicing always in his presence, rejoicing in his whole world and delighting in mankind."

Because Christ lives in us, those verses are ours! We can be filled with delight day after day. Let's emphasize that: *We can be filled with* delight *day after day.* And those things that can and will delight us have nothing to do with position or ministry or fascinating things to do. We can have delight in the dull, monotonous months, in the routine, mundane days, in the lean, hungry years.

Three things will bring rejoicing to our souls: (1) God's very presence, (2) His world around us, and (3) people! God's promise to be present with us always can bring us comfort and delight. So can the complexity and variety of His creation: a flower, the misty rain, the billowing clouds. Sometimes we may have to look hard into some of the people we encounter, but as we ask, God will help us delight in them, too. These are three pools of delight we can bathe in when we're young and strong, old and feeble, or incapacitated or ill.

Anytime. Anyplace. Any condition.

I'll probably have to remind myself often when dullness of soul creeps over me, but the truth is that God provides . . . *no excuse for boredom*!

---

*Father, when I feel disgruntled — dissatisfied with the "ordinary" life You've given me — please remind me that my circumstances aren't necessarily the problem. When I feel like a plug has been pulled from the bottom of my soul and all the meaning has disappeared down a dark drain, remind me to look for Your delights — Your purpose in my everyday life — until I find fresh joy in Your presence, Your world, and Your people.*

Then our mouth was filled with laughter,
And our tongue with joyful shouting:

Then they said among the nations,
"The LORD has done great things for them."
The LORD has done great things for us;
We are glad. (Psalm 126:2-3, NASB)

How great is your goodness,
    which you have stored up for those who fear you.
        (Psalm 31:19)

# SIX

# Sip and Savor

------◆------

*I* reached into the cupboard for a mug, filled it with water, and popped it into the microwave—only vaguely aware of again picking one of the three mugs that represent significant relationships in my life.

One declares, "Jesus cares for you."

A second—which my husband gave me some time ago—says, "The Exceptional Woman" and on the inner lip is a heart and another message saying, "You're Sensational." (That one makes me feel especially good on dreary mornings!)

A third—given to me by a special friend—states, "Friends are forever."

I find myself using one of those three cups almost every morning even though another dozen rest on the shelf.

After the water was piping hot, I mixed in a packet of hot chocolate—sugar-free, of course—then carefully carried it to a little bedroom-study where I have my time with the Lord. I sat on the couch with my Bible and sipped that very hot liquid, savoring every swallow.

One morning a couple of months ago, it dawned on me that what I was doing with my morning hot chocolate was *exactly* what I should do with the Word of God. I should "sip and savor" it.

As I sip and savor the chocolate, it goes down into my innards, is absorbed, and becomes a part of me. I feel nour-

ished by it. So also should it be with God's Word.
Only *more*. Much, much more.

---

So often I am content with so little, when God wants to give me so much!

Recently I puzzled over this passage in Isaiah 55:

"Come, all you who are thirsty,
    come to the waters;
and you who have no money,
    come, buy and eat!
Come, buy wine and milk
    without money and without cost.
Why spend money on what is not bread,
    and your labor on what does not satisfy?
Listen, listen to me, and eat what is good,
    and your soul will delight in the richest of fare."
        (verses 1-2)

This Scripture exhorts the thirsty to do three things: *come, buy,* and *eat*. We don't need any money to "buy," so all we have to do is come and ask for the two things mentioned here—wine and milk. But why specifically wine and milk?

A glimmer began to grow into the light of understanding. Milk represents what we need for health, for life, for sustenance—the *needs* in life. On the other hand, wine is used in Scripture for celebrations, feasts, joy, and (so it seems to me) not for what we need to have but what we want to have—the *extra desires* in life.

As a mother, I was obligated to meet my daughter's *needs*. But what a joy it was when I could delight her heart by giving her some of the fun stuff too—surprises, a few things I knew she wanted, extras—just for pure pleasure.

Our Father's giving is like that—only much, much more! He is the perfect parent, and in this passage He declares that He wants to supply *both* our needs and our wants—what we need for health and what is for pure joy. God does indeed delight to delight each of us.

Oh, He isn't going to give us what He knows will harm us—even if we ask for it. He won't give us what would spoil us or indulge our flesh. But, as the God who knows all things, who does all things well, who is an all-loving Father, He longs for us to ask Him for *everything*—for "daily bread," certainly, and whatever will meet our needs. But He also *asks* that we ask for the extra serendipities that He takes great pleasure in giving us as well.

Now, I get excited about that!

*Dear Lord, I am awed by Your wonder. When I think of Your holiness, I don't understand how You can bless me.*

*But when I think of Your greatness, I realize You cannot fail to bless me.*

*And when I think of Your love, I know You will not fail to bless me.*

*How wonderful You are. Thank You.*

> "The mountains will drip new wine,
>     and the hills will flow with milk;
>     all the ravines of Judah will run with water.
> A fountain will flow out of the LORD's house
>     and will water the valley of acacias." (Joel 3:18)

PART TWO

# He Transforms My Weariness

*You are a shield around me, O LORD;*
*you bestow glory on me*
*and lift up my head.*
PSALM 3:3

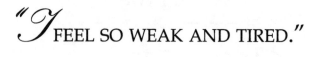

"*I* FEEL SO WEAK AND TIRED."

IT'S A FEELING WE ADMIT EITHER
ALOUD OR IN OUR HEADS. WEARINESS
IS A PART OF MOST OF OUR LIVES.

I'M GLAD THAT JESUS UNDERSTANDS
MY FATIGUE. I'M EVEN MORE GLAD
THAT HE HAS MADE PROMISES
CONCERNING IT. HE HAS SAID,
"MY GRACE IS SUFFICIENT FOR YOU,
FOR MY POWER IS MADE PERFECT IN
WEAKNESS" (2 CORINTHIANS 12:9).

AND THEREBY, HE *TRANSFORMS* MY
WEARINESS. . . . REALLY.

# SEVEN

# Lessons from My Word Processor

typed the word "END" and pressed the key to store the several pages I'd just finished writing on the disk. Suddenly words flashed onto the computer screen:

DISK FULL!!!
DISK FULL!!!
DISK FULL!!!

*"Oh, no!"* I groaned and reached for my manual to try to find out how to delete something in order to make room for what I'd just written. I felt like kicking myself around the block when I failed and had to start all over typing on another disk.

Later, I realized how often my life is like that! There are times when too much of *everything* has been put into my circuits. Words flash in my mind: "DISK FULL!!! DISK FULL!!! DISK FULL!!!" and life abruptly shatters out of control.

With the computer and with my life, the problem of overload is solved by *deleting*. Getting a computer with more capacity resolved one problem, but being unable to trade in my life for one with more capacity, I find that I must constantly work to delete the nonessentials.

Sometimes it isn't so much a matter of being on overload as it is a matter of being overwhelmed. I feel overwhelmed when a day, a job, or even life is too much for me.

31

The Christian missionary Jim Elliott said, "God's will is always bigger than you bargain for." *Often* I find myself in a situation where I say to the Father, "Lord, what have You gotten us into this time?" and the Father invariably answers, "Nothing I can't handle!"

I'm finally recognizing that God refuses to put my life into neat little packages that I can easily manage all by myself. My "In" basket rarely reads, "Carole Can Handle." Instead it's often, "Impossible Tasks."

And there is a reason.

Only when I feel inadequate do I rely on *God* to be my adequacy. Only when I know I'm not sufficient for a task, do I depend on Him to be my only sufficiency. Only *then* do I cry, "Help!" and experience the promise of 2 Corinthians 12:9—"My grace is sufficient for you, for my power is made perfect in weakness."

Being overloaded is bad.

Being overwhelmed is good.

When I'm on overload, I must pause and delete nonessentials in my life. But when I'm overwhelmed . . . that is the time to revel in my weakness, to acknowledge my helplessness, to glory in my inability, and to once again know and understand that, indeed, I *am* nothing. But God . . . *God is everything I need.*

---

*Father, help me to discern when the pressures of life seem to overtake me, whether the reason is being overloaded or overwhelmed. When I'm overloaded, give me wisdom to delete the nonessentials in my life. And when I'm feeling overwhelmed, help me to understand and experience that Your strength is made perfect in my weakness.*

Being confident of this, that he who began a good work in you will carry it on to completion until the day of Christ Jesus. (Philippians 1:6)

EIGHT

# *Weary of Warfare*

felt as if two incredibly strong blows had landed in my solar plexus leaving me doubled over and groaning in pain.

First, a tearful telephone call from my brother telling me that his son had been crushed to death that morning on a conveyer belt at work, leaving a distraught widow and three young children. Then a blur of changed plans. Rushed flights. Weeping loved ones. Bewildered children. Tears. The funeral procession. Disjointed conversations. Tears. Flowers. Frazzled nerves. Little sleep. Concerned friends. Tears.

Several tortured days later, I flew home and walked into the comfort of my husband's strong arms.

Three days afterward, the second punch landed as I rushed Jack to the hospital with a life-threatening twelve-inch blood clot in his leg.

Another blurred week ensued. Clutching fear. Long hours in the tiny, claustrophobic hospital room. Ruptured plans. Questioning future. Visiting friends. Sleeping alone. Tears. Numbness. Weakness. Helplessness.

I desperately needed help . . . to have strength, joy, and grace. Actually, help for *everything*.

I reached for my Bible as if I were a drowning person clutching a life raft and began reading where I'd left off — 2 Chronicles 14. I puzzled over what King Asa's dilemma could have to do with my situation and read with increasing wonder. King Asa faced a life-threatening, destructive, scary plight as a mighty army of Cushites confronted him and threatened to wipe his nation from the earth.

I could identify with that!

I read Asa's prayer once, twice, then a third time and marveled. And then . . . I read it as mine. My additions to the eleventh verse went something like this:

> Lord, there is no one like You to help the powerless . . . (Father, that's *me*! I'm powerless against my own emotions, my weakness, my fears. I'm powerless against the overwhelming sorrows of my dear ones, and I'm powerless against the forces that wage war in Jack's body) . . . to help the powerless against the mighty. (That's my situation too, Lord. The forces — of the unknown, of aging, of pressures, of confusion, of sorrow and anger, of evil — You name it and it's a mighty army in my life right now!)
>
> Help us for we rely on You. Don't let man prevail against . . .

I thought surely the next word would be *me* or *us*. The picture came to mind of a great horde of troops and chariots swooping over the hill while a small defenseless person stood in the valley waiting for them to strike, helpless to put up any kind of fight. Weak and shaking, the person raises trembling arms to Heaven and cries, "If anyone is up there, *I need help*."

But the verse doesn't say, "Don't let man prevail against *me*." No! Instead, it says, "Don't let man prevail against *You*."

*Ahhh.* Now, the picture changes dramatically and wonderfully. The same mighty army sweeps over the hill, but suddenly — over the opposite hill — comes a giant, so enormous he blots out the light of the horizon, putting fear in the hearts of the attackers. The giant is indestructible. He is all-powerful. He is invincible. He is God.

And you know where that helpless person (me) is? Why, I'm snuggled in a small see-through-to-the-outside breast pocket *close to His heart!*

I clutched my Bible close to myself and wept. Not tears of helplessness or pain this time, but tears of joy and thanksgiving.

The blows of life can and do leave me doubled over with pain and weakness. *But not for long.* Not when God, through His precious Word, pours His strength and joy and grace into my life. Not when He shows me how I'm carried . . . close to His heart!

*Father, help me to remember that when troubles flood in and I'm weak and powerless against everything, You are my shield. You are my hiding place . . . and You carry me close to Your heart.*

> In a desert land he found him,
>     in a barren and howling waste.
> He shielded him and cared for him;
>     he guarded him as the apple of his eye,
> like an eagle that stirs up its nest
>     and hovers over its young,
> that spreads its wings to catch them
>     and carries them on its pinions.
> The LORD alone led him. (Deuteronomy 32:10-12)

# NINE

# In the Face of Betrayal

*T*he small mountain of Kleenex mounted beside me on the couch—evidence of and debris from my pain.

A close friend had betrayed me. Over the weeks, I'd managed to deal with it and forgive, even though she hadn't asked. A wall of denial on her part blocked the kind of deep communication we'd previously shared, and finally, I accepted that too.

"Lord, I'm struggling once again. The problem isn't forgiveness or acceptance. It is the difficulty of handling the relationship *now*. She seems content with a level of friendship that is shallow to me. I've tried several times, but she won't talk about it anymore, so we've not *resolved* this ugly thing. What should I do? Should I be polite but distant? Should I smile, but pass her by?

"I feel as if I've been robbed of something precious and valuable. And I don't know how to handle the relationship from this point. Lord, please help me."

I reached for another tissue as I opened my Bible to Matthew 26, my chapter for the day. I think God arranged before the foundation of the world for me to read those particular verses on that particular day in order to give me an answer to my question. That morning He showed me how Christ Himself handled both friends who let Him down totally and one who actually betrayed Him.

Christ was deeply troubled, so much so that His soul

was "overwhelmed with sorrow to the point of death." As far as we know, this was the only time He ever shared such a need with His disciples. Urgently, He begged Peter, James, and John to watch and pray with Him and for Him.

Instead, they went to sleep.

He rebuked them and begged again.

They went to sleep.

The third time when He found them sleeping, He didn't wake them but returned to pray . . . alone.

I had read Matthew 26:36-45 many times before, but suddenly God blazed a new truth into my soul. I felt Christ's anguish and His disappointment in His friends for their failure to help Him at such a time. Yet He loved them so much He placed their need for rest (in preparation for the coming violent days) above His own overwhelming sorrow. What supernatural love and concern!

I prayed, "Lord Jesus, Your friends disappointed You. They let You down. They failed You. But in spite of that, Your love and concern for them never wavered for one moment."

My tears dried up somewhat, and the words in the next paragraph focused clearly.

I knew what was coming, of course. Judas, determined to pursue his own selfish ends, arrived with the crowd to betray the Lord with a kiss! Jesus had predicted it. He understood exactly what was about to happen. They had walked the roads of Judea together for over three years. Judas had watched Jesus heal the blind and the leprous, raise the dead, and provide for needs. Jesus had given Himself to Judas in friendship. He knew this was the one who would betray Him to His death. He'd even said to the other disciples, "Here comes my betrayer" (verse 46).

Then Judas came up to Him out of the crowd, greeted Him, and kissed Him.

What would you or I have done at that moment?

Most of us would have vehemently hurled accusations at him. "Betrayer!" "Traitor!" "Informer!"

Those who could have stifled their anger and hurt might have merely said, "Judas," acknowledging his presence with sadness.

But the first word out of the Lord's mouth was "*Friend*"! The second gave His permission for the act of betrayal!

He said, "*Friend*, do what you came for."

That was all!

And the soldiers arrested Jesus.

My tears erupted again. Only these were tears of release and joy, for I had my answer!

Both to the disciples who disappointed and failed Him and to Judas who betrayed Him, Christ extended consistent and constant *love*. Regardless of their actions, He demonstrated His love through His words and deeds. And since He is to be my example, then that is to be my response as well.

---

*Lord Jesus, fill my heart with Your perfect love so that my greatest concern will be showing Your character to everyone — even to those who hurt or betray me — whether or not they ask.*

> Be kind and compassionate to one another, forgiving each other, just as in Christ God forgave you.
> (Ephesians 4:32)

# TEN

# Weariness

—————➤◄◄———

Our daughter, Lynn, arrived in Colorado Springs from her home in Mexico tired. Fog in Los Angeles had delayed her flight for five hours, robbing her of a night's sleep.

She entered our home looking bedraggled and weary, and moaned, "I just want to flop and have some TLC!" (As most of you know, that stands for Tender Loving Care.)

I replied sympathetically, "Well, you don't have to do *anything* here — and you can do *that* very slowly."

When am I going to practice what I preach?

I rarely do *anything* slowly. Generally, I'm doing three or four things at once (just ask Jack!). I read a book and iron or unload the dishwasher at the same time I'm watching the news on television (when I take *time* to watch the news that is). Since our kids gave us a cordless phone for Christmas, I can even unload the dryer and fold clothes while talking to a friend (the cord wouldn't reach before). And I say to myself, "Isn't this great?" *But is it?*

If somehow I can discipline my body to be still, my mind keeps right on going and often "worries" a matter the way a dog worries a rag, pulling and chewing on it until there isn't much left. Frequently, all this frantic activity leaves me worn and exhausted. I wonder where the peace and quiet went, and occasionally I even long for the carefree days of long ago.

Yesterday, I observed a young child in the mall, laughing and running without a concern in the world. When she suddenly drooped, as small children will, her father picked her up, positioned her head so it rested on his shoulder and carried her. She went instantly and soundly to sleep.

I really wouldn't want to be two years old again. But sometimes I think it would be grand to experience that pressure-free existence when Mom and Dad took care of *everything*.

On one of my draggy, dreary days God showed me that He does exactly that! Even though my gray hairs now outnumber the brown, God still cares for me as His *child*.

I read the following passage slowly, then inwardly shouted, *Hallelujah!* Isaiah 46:3-4 says, "Listen to me . . . you whom I have upheld since you were conceived, and have carried since your birth. Even to your old age and gray hairs I am he, I am he who will sustain you. I have made you and I will carry you; I will sustain you and I will rescue you."

I grabbed a pen and paper and scribbled:

God *upholds* me when I am about to fall.
When I am despondent and discouraged,
    He's the "lifter of my head."
He *carries* me when I have no strength of my own,
    when I am helpless,
    and for all of my life—from birth to death.
He *sustains* me when I am weary, worn out,
    when those I love, can't,
    when friends turn away,
    when support systems collapse.
He *rescues* me when fear overtakes me,
    when enemies surround me.
What a fantastic Father!

Such insight came home to me then! When I am exhausted and feeling fragile and alone and not able to do so much as lift my head, God will supply me not only with His tender loving care and with His rest but also with a peace of heart that tells me I can do even that *very slowly!*

*Father, how wonderful it is to know that You carry me! I'm so glad to be able to snuggle in Your arms and know I can rest there securely. My mind knows that. Please, help my heart to feel it, too.*

> He tends his flock like a shepherd:
>> He gathers the lambs in his arms
> and carries them close to his heart;
>> he gently leads those that have young.
>>> (Isaiah 40:11)

# ELEVEN

# Limp No Longer

With great difficulty, each day he limped along the path, climbing painfully around the boulders that blocked his way. Crevices — some deep — caused him to stumble and sometimes fall. Not long ago, he had stumbled into one and broken his leg, which caused his present limp.

"Walking this rough path every day certainly doesn't help the healing process," he told himself as he maneuvered carefully over some particularly formidable spots.

Still, he had no choice. It was the one and only road, and so, each day, he agonizingly made his way.

Then one morning, he slipped and fell in thick mud, and brambles scratched deep gashes on his arms. He said to himself, "This is foolish! I have to walk this path every day for the rest of my life! I've simply got to do something to make it easier."

He sought the help of a friend who owned a forklift, and together, sweating and straining, they removed several huge boulders that lay directly in his path, which he would've had to climb around. He rented a bulldozer and filled in the deepest gullies. Now as he walked the path, he carried a shovel to pack in the cracks and ruts, and a garden rake to take care of the smaller mounds and knolls.

And, after many days, the path he walked became level.

Of course, maintenance was always a problem. Small rock slides, storms, and occasional vandalism required more cleanup. But the repairs were easy compared to the initial work of making the path smooth and even.

That picture came to mind as I pondered two verses of Scripture. Hebrews 12:12-13 states, "Strengthen your feeble arms and weak knees. 'Make level paths for your feet,' so that the lame may not be disabled, but rather healed." The verses puzzled me. I could strengthen my feeble arms and weak knees (that's a word picture if I've ever heard one!) through spending time knowing the Bible and talking with God in prayer. But how do I make level paths for my feet? These verses indicated that I was to clear my own path so that, even if I was lame before, I would heal completely and walk more easily.

I found the answer to my "Yes, but how?" in the very next verses.

The first instruction is to make every effort to live in peace with all people and to be holy (verse 14). When I'm at odds with those around me, inevitably I'm going to stumble, fall, and get all banged up. Anger that isn't dealt with, along with known sin in my life, are like boulders, rocks, and washouts that obstruct my path, and I must remove them.

The second guideline is just as difficult. I am to "see to it . . . that no bitter root grows up to cause trouble and defile many" (verse 15). I have been crippled by this boulder more than once! Although I'll need help to eliminate it, it must be done.

The third command is to "see that no one is sexually immoral, or is godless" (verse 16). Falling into the fissure of immorality could cripple me for life, so at all costs, I am to avoid it.

Enormous commands! And impossible except that God provides the forklifts, bulldozers, and shovels to level the path I walk each day — through the lift of a friend to whom I'm accountable, by the rakes and shovels of daily obedience to His Word, asking for direction and the help of the Holy Spirit.

Another major piece of equipment that God frequently uses to help me work at leveling my path is His *discipline*, which is described in Hebrews 12:5 as a "word of encouragement"! I think of encouragement as a cheerful word, a compliment, help in lifting a load. But somehow the encouragement of discipline escaped me until I really began to think about it. A child finds security in knowing he has limits and boundaries — rules are there for his protection. David looked on God's rod as "comfort" in Psalm 23. It is a "word of encouragement" to know that God will rebuke me, correct me, and instruct me if and when I stray or deliberately choose to step off His path.

Yes, God provides the means with which to make the path level, but the *will* to smooth out the path is mine.

I read the verse again slowly: "Strengthen your feeble arms and weak knees. 'Make level paths for your feet.'" Could I do that? *Would* I do that?

A formidable boulder obstructing my path is my own nature. I have that kind of personality that doesn't like to say no. And even if I've said no, some little persistent voice inside keeps bringing up a hundred things I ought to do. I need wisdom to discern between God's commands — no boulders to make me stumble there — and my own "I should's," which cause exhaustion, worry, and stress and make me fall every time.

---

*Father, You have commanded me to make level paths for my feet and have given me the Holy Spirit to help me do that. Lord, as the psalmist prayed, I too pray: "O Lord, lead me in Thy righteousness ... make Thy way straight before me."*
*And now, Lord, help me to obey!*

They will come with weeping;
    they will pray as I bring them back.
I will lead them beside streams of water
    on a level path where they will not stumble.
        (Jeremiah 31:9)

PART THREE

# He Thrills At My Trust

*My flesh and my heart may fail,*
*but God is the strength of my heart*
*and my portion forever.*
PSALM 73:26

*S*OMEONE HAS SAID THAT MUCH OF THE CHRISTIAN LIFE IS JUST HANGING ON! WE COULD ARGUE ABOUT THE "MUCH," BUT CERTAINLY SOME OF OUR DAYS FALL INTO THAT CATEGORY.

"I WILL TRUST GOD NO MATTER WHAT" BECOMES THE RECOURSE FOR DAYS OF WEARINESS AND FATIGUE. KNOWING THAT UNDERNEATH ARE HIS EVERLASTING ARMS, EVEN WHEN WE DON'T FEEL HIM. KNOWING THAT WE ARE SHELTERED IN HIS LOVE, EVEN WHEN WE DON'T SENSE IT.

TRUSTING HIM . . . *ANYHOW.*

# TWELVE

# The Gathering

On a warm September Saturday in Atlanta, Mike gathered his family around him for a short Bible study. He said to his sons, ages five and eight, "You know Daddy has a tumor growing on his thigh. Sunday the church is going to have a prayer meeting to ask God to heal me. But if God chooses not to do that, I'll have to have it cut away next month. It may grow back. And if it does, I'll die."

Little John Michael's eyes clouded with alarm as Mike continued, "I want to read you something that God wrote down for us in the book of Hebrews: 'It is appointed for men to die once' [9:27, NASB]. God *appoints* the time we die. That means He decides when it will happen. I won't die one second before His appointment. Remember that."

Eight-year-old Daniel nodded his fair head vigorously as he comprehended what his daddy was saying.

I wiped away a tear as my nephew Mike told me over the phone about that incident. I stood in awe as I looked courage in the face. And once again, as with my sister (his mother) who died of leukemia at age forty-eight, as with my father who died at fifty-seven, also of leukemia, I was forced to take out the package labeled "death" and examine it closely.

Death looks ugly and frightening to most of us. But the Bible doesn't present it that way. I read about Jacob of whom it is written, "He . . . breathed his last and was gathered to his people" (Genesis 49:33). And I wrote:

Oh Father,
What a beautiful phrase You used when Jacob died.
   "He was gathered to his people."
   Gathered means "brought in."
What a picture of heaven!
   Gathered to loved ones gone ahead.
Tenderly gathered . . . joyously brought in,
   ushered in with ceremony as the "honored guest."
Met by Abraham and Sarah,
   Isaac and Rebekah,
   his own dear Rachel and Leah,
   and a host of others.
But welcomed first . . . by You.
He was one of Your people
   and You must have been a part of *his* "people" as
     well.
Why is death something we fear?
It will be a *gathering* together of *our* people!
How comforting. How blessed!

After prayers for healing, Mike's operation was successful. The tumor was nonmalignant. God willing, Mike will be with us for some years, and I'm grateful. Because death here and now *does* have a sting. The verse, "Where, O death, is your victory? Where, O death, is your sting?" (1 Corinthians 15:55), is often taken out of context. We snatch it from its setting, as described in verse 54: "When the perishable has been clothed with the imperishable, and the mortal with immortality, then the saying that is written will come true: 'Death has been swallowed up in victory.'"

Christians have a hope. Christians have an inheritance. Christians have a comforter. But death, right now in this lifetime, does sting. We grieve at our loss. We weep with pain. But *someday*, when Christ comes again, *then* there will be no more sting in death.

But in the midst of present suffering and incalculable loss, when death happens — to Mike, to me — for that person it will be a glorious *gathering*. A joyous homecoming. A splendid reunion.

May we be reminded of that. And, in the midst of our sorrow, may we remember the homegoer's joy. And *rejoice*.

*Father, thank You for speaking of death so joyously — as a "gathering," as a time of reward, of no more tears, of a Heaven we can't begin to comprehend. May the fear of the pain and process of dying be overshadowed by the anticipation of my heart and mind that death is a time of reunion and joy.*

The body that is sown is perishable, it is raised imperishable; it is sown in dishonor, it is raised in glory; it is sown in weakness, it is raised in power; it is sown a natural body, it is raised a spiritual body. (1 Corinthians 15:42-44)

# The Door

*M*y brother Kent was a tall not-quite-five-year-old with hair that a comb and water could not tame.

He'd been on the couch for several minutes, scrutinizing the picture of Jesus knocking at a door. When Mother finally sank down beside him, Kent questioned, "Mommy, what is Jesus doin'?"

Mother replied, "Well, Kent, Jesus is knocking at the door of a heart. Jesus wants to come in and live with each one of us for always and be our friend, taking care of us and forgiving us for all the bad things we do.

"But notice, son, that there isn't a handle on the outside of the door. Each person has to open the door of his or her life—his heart—from the inside and invite Jesus to come in. He is a gentleman and would never force Himself into anyone's life."

Kent pondered that awhile, then asked, "Mommy, are there people who don't ask Jesus to come in?"

"Well, Kent, some people leave Him standing outside a very long time. And yes, others never let Him come in."

Kent was distressed at such a thought. After several more moments, he took a deep breath and let it out slowly. Then he said, "Well! I'm not goin' to leave Jesus standing outside *my* heart. I'm goin' to let Him in *right now*."

He placed his small fist at the side of his chest and made

a motion of opening a door. Then aloud he said, "Jesus, please come into my heart *right now*."

He waited a minute and, in a sweeping gesture, closed the door and with a beaming smile exclaimed, "There! Now I'm Jesus' boy; aren't I, Mommy?"

And he was!

Early in our lives, Mother made it clear to each of us that we needed Jesus. Though I had been born into a family who loved God, that fact didn't make me one of His children. God has no grandchildren, only *children*.

Mom had carefully explained to us that we all had done a lot of things that deserved to be punished. If we did only one wrong thing a day — times 365 days in a year, multiplied by how old we were — our hearts were black with sin, separating us from God's perfect Heaven. (As young as we were, we could understand that if *we* went there, it wouldn't be perfect anymore!)

But she explained that although the wages or payment of all that sin is death — spiritual death, which is separation from God Himself — He offers us the gift of "eternal life in Jesus Christ our Lord" (Romans 6:23).

We knew the facts early. God had sent His only Son to earth, not only to tell us about the Father, but to live a perfect life (as God, He could do that!), so that at the end of His life, He didn't have to die for His own sins. He didn't *have* any sins, so He could take the place of another person who did.

And that is exactly what He did! He — the One who never sinned — took upon Himself my sin. And not only mine, but the sin of the whole world.

My part was simple. I only had to receive the gift already given. And when I did that, I became one of God's children — a Christ-one!

I opened the door of my life to the Creator of the universe, Jesus Christ, a few years after Kent, and Christ changed my life.

I too could say, "There! Now I'm Jesus' girl; aren't I, Mommy?"

And I was.

Have been ever since.

*Lord Jesus, You've always known the condition of my heart. I want to thank You for coming into my life and changing me. Thank You for giving Yourself to pay the penalty for my sin.*

*(Or perhaps, you'll want to open that door to Him, if you have not done so before.)*

This is the testimony: God has given us eternal life, and this life is in his Son. He who has the Son has life; he who does not have the Son of God does not have life. (1 John 5:11-12)

# FOURTEEN

# Temptation

——————◆————————

*L*ynn, age fourteen months, sat in the bathtub under my watchful eye. Suddenly, she snatched the soap and put it to her mouth. When I repossessed it, she screamed in protest, offended that her mother would take that appetizing, slippery, pink, delicious morsel away!

Again and again she tried to put it to her mouth. Over and over I took it from her. Again and again she screamed in protest.

At last I decided to let her learn the hard way. The next time she grabbed the soap, I watched quietly. Opening her mouth wide, she took a huge bite and looked delighted — for a short moment! Then her face screwed up and she started spitting and crying — not in anger this time, but in distress.

In the scramble that followed, she got soap in her eyes, came perilously close to being momentarily submerged, and gagged. I felt as bad as Lynn did concerning the whole incident.

Lynn never again tried to eat soap.

Sometimes . . . God takes the soap away before we bite into it. And we scream in anger. Sometimes . . . He lets us eat the soap. And then we scream in distress.

Today . . . being eons away from the "twenty-something" of those days when Lynn was fourteen months old, I look back with wonder . . . at the time God said a definite "*no*" to buying a house that I just *knew* was perfect for us . . . and how I pouted. The year He said *"no"* to an overseas trip I desperately wanted to make with Jack . . . and I glowered.

Then I remembered a year later discovering the location of that "perfect house" had become extremely undesirable. I reflected on the timing of that trip and realized that because God said "no" I was home to say goodbye to Mom when she went to Heaven.

And I marveled at the goodness of the Father.

One morning I read, "You [God] open your hand and satisfy the desires of every living thing" (Psalm 145:16), and a mental picture popped into my head. A huge closed fist was reaching down to me, while I eagerly waited for the hand to open. I expected it to contain serendipities, happiness, joy, health, security, and loving people for my life.

The fist opened slowly, and I held my breath. But then I gasped because there was *nothing* in the hand . . . nothing that is, but the *hand itself*. I was struck by the truth of *The Living Bible*'s paraphrase of Psalm 23:1 — "Because the Lord is my Shepherd, I have everything I need!"

Of course. God opens His hand and offers me Himself! And He is my joy, my security, my love, my everything! He really is all I need.

So how come I want to eat soap?

———◆·◆———

*Father, thank You. Thank You for saying "no" when I was begging for "yes." And forgive me for complaining! Thank You for remaining firm in Your refusal to let me put that soap into my mouth, causing me to spit and gag!*

*Thank You for being the perfect parent.*

*I know that You do all things well . . . and so, may I accept from Your hand what is good. May I not desire what is not.*

He gave them their request:
    but sent leanness into their soul. (Psalm 106:15, KJV)

# FIFTEEN

# How Much Do You Really Want?

he sun splashed in bright puddles of light on the kitchen counter, but we were too absorbed to notice. We'd been talking about commitment, and Lynn mused, "You know, in college I remember hearing a sermon on 'Do you really want what you really want?' and I've never forgotten it."

I raised my eyebrows questioningly, "That sounds like a strange one."

"Not really," she countered. "I can still remember it because it was so thought provoking in several areas."

"Such as?" I prompted.

"Well, Do we want to serve God enough to pay the price? Do we want a loving marriage enough to work hard for it? Do we want humility even at the cost of humiliation? Do we want to live a life of sacrifice without sacrificing?"

I got the picture.

The rest of the day those concepts buzzed around in my head. I say I want to know the deep truth of God's Word. But do I want it enough to spend the time it takes, the energy it uses, the sacrifice it demands? I say I want to end my life well, but do I want it enough to discipline my body, my mind, my spirit? I say that I want to give more time to prayer, but. . . .

And there's more. Do I really want the *results* of what I really want?

Early in our days with The Navigators, someone told us that Daws Trotman (founder of our ministry) — realizing he was often brusque and unrelenting—prayed that God would soften his heart. Not long afterward, a son was born to Daws and his wife, Lila, who was severely handicapped both mentally and physically. And that son caused a deep change in Dawson's personality.

A different man, a missionary, prayed that God would work in his life to make him more gentle. A few weeks later his beloved wife died suddenly of a brain aneurysm, leaving behind three young children. His testimony years later was that God used his wife's death to break him and mold him to be more like the Master.

Jim Elliot once wrote, "God's will is always bigger than you bargain for." And, I might add, *different* from the picture in my mind.

I think that a lot of us pray for characteristics such as love, patience, and gentleness to be built into our lives, but we would like to take back that request when God brings difficult circumstances to produce those very characteristics in us. Then we'd like to shout, "I didn't mean it, Lord! Erase that one!"

But God takes us at our word. He brings fire into our lives—so hot it melts us, molds us, breaks us. Only from the vantage point of later years, or perhaps in some cases from eternity itself, can we say, "Thank You for taking me at my word. I really did want what I really wanted in spite of what I had to go through for You to get it there."

Think about it.

Do *you* really want what you really want? And do you really want the *results* of what you really want?

---

*Oh, Lord! Help me. May I really want what I really want and be willing to accept the results of how You make that happen in my life. And may I want it . . . enough.*

I want to know Christ and the power of his resurrection and the fellowship of sharing in his sufferings, becoming like him in his death. . . . One thing I do:

Forgetting what is behind and straining toward what is ahead, I press on toward the goal to win the prize for which God has called me heavenward in Christ Jesus. (Philippians 3:10,13-14)

For it is God who works in you to will and to act according to his good purpose. (Philippians 2:13)

# SIXTEEN

# No Power

$\mathcal{T}$he guest room — done in blue with its own bath —
was inviting but cold. By the time I unpacked my small suitcase, got ready for bed, and shook out an Excedrin P.M. for
a slight nagging headache, my feet were freezing. Knowing
that after a stimulating and exhausting weekend women's
conference — too much to eat and too much caffeine — it would
be difficult enough to sleep even *without* cold feet, I tried
everything to get them warm. Rubbed them. Put my slip-
pers on. Rubbed them again.

Nothing worked.

The late March wind whistled through the eaves.
Defeated and shivering, I crawled into the bed, drew my feet
up as close to my body as I could, and tried to sleep. For
three hours I tossed and turned, wondering why the medication hadn't cleared the headache or helped me relax, and
finally fell into a restless sleep.

The next morning as I groggily smoothed the covers of
the double bed, I glanced down at the floor and saw a familiar cord pushed almost out of sight under the bed. I drew it
out and discovered that the cold bed I'd slept on had an electric blanket, ready to be turned on to make the bed toasty
and warm. I groaned.

Then I went into the bathroom to brush my teeth, glanced
down at the countertop, and discovered the pill laying there
where I'd put it. I groaned again.

An electric blanket can't warm me unless I turn it on. A medication can't get rid of a headache and help me relax unless I take it.

Then I glanced at my Bible resting on top of my suitcase and smiled as the analogy struck me. I realized full well that I'd just been shown a truth we'd talked about that week-end — graphically. God won't answer prayers that I don't pray. The Word of God can't revive me, make me wise, or give me direction unless I open it.

---

*Lord, often my needs are much deeper than a lost night's sleep. I fail to appropriate what You have already provided. Forgive me. And help me to know that all I have to do is reach out and receive.*

Open my eyes that I may see
    wonderful things in your law. . . .
Your statutes are my delight;
    they are my counselors. . . .
My comfort in my suffering is this:
    Your promise preserves my life. . . .
It was good for me to be afflicted
    so that I might learn your decrees. . . .
May your unfailing love be my comfort,
    according to your promise to your servant. . . .
My heart is set on keeping your decrees
    to the very end. (Psalm 119:18,24,50,71,76,112)

# SEVENTEEN

# Listening to God

She crouched beside my chair during the final meal of the women's retreat, her brows drawn together in concern and concentration. "I just have to know," she said. "*How* does God talk to you?"

Her question was insightful, and suddenly I was aware of using, but never explaining, that idea during the retreat. And this newly born believer earnestly wanted to know how God speaks to His children.

I thought for a long moment, then said, "For me, He speaks by a distinct impression in my heart. He's never spoken to me aloud, but sometimes the thought that He puts in my soul is so vivid that He might as well have! Many times it is just a thought or an idea that flashes into my mind and I know it is from Him."

She nodded, and we talked for a few minutes more before she returned to her table.

Later I considered her question more thoroughly.

How do I know it is God speaking and not my own thoughts answering me? Could Satan put thoughts into my head? How am I sure of what God says? Valid questions, every one.

God is the same yesterday, today, and forever. He spoke in a number of ways in times past—through prophets, angels, visions, through the consciences of men, and aloud as He did to Moses at the burning bush. Today, while He communicates with us primarily through His Word, He certainly isn't limited to that.

If God's thoughts toward me every day are more in number than the sand (see Psalm 139:17-18) and since His Holy Spirit dwells in me, He wants to communicate with me, as any two people would who love each other.

David said, "You [God] guide me with your counsel" (Psalm 73:24), and he also prayed, "Let the morning bring me word of your unfailing love, for I have put my trust in you. Show me the way I should go, for to you I lift up my soul" (143:8). These and many other passages convince me that the Lord does speak if we open our ears to hear Him.

Can Satan deceive us into thinking it is God who is speaking when it is really the enemy of our souls? Yes, but Satan generally whispers evil things that are contrary to God's Word. And we know that God speaks only what agrees with His written Word. If I'm unsure as to whether an idea is from Satan, or even my own thoughts talking, I disregard the message and continue to pray for clarity.

How does God speak? For me He speaks in various ways.

Sometimes a thought pops into my mind—a thought so different from what I was thinking, or so creative I never would have thought of it, or opposite to what I *wanted* God to say to me. When that happens—and it lines up with God's Word—I know I've heard His voice in a distinctive way.

Many times He speaks through a verse of Scripture. As I'm reading, one verse will seem to reach out, grab me by the shoulders, give me a little shake, and command, *"Take special note!"*

But often God and I have quite a conversation together simply by my hearing His still, small voice speaking quietly through an impression to my inner self. What an encouragement it is when I tell Him, "I love You, Lord," and I hear His whisper, "And *you* are My beloved."

I pray frequently that I'll hear His voice more often and

more clearly. When I don't, I know He hasn't stopped speaking, rather, *I have stopped listening.*

---

*Father, thank You for all the ways You speak to me; for Your Word and for Your Holy Spirit speaking to my heart. I want to hear You more. Help me, Lord, to listen.*

> Listen and hear my voice;
>> pay attention and hear what I say. (Isaiah 28:23)

> Whether you turn to the right or to the left, your ears will hear a voice behind you, saying, "This is the way; walk in it." (30:21)

> The ears of those who hear will listen. (32:3)

PART FOUR

# He Touches My Hopelessness

*Don't fear anything except the Lord of the armies of heaven! If you fear him, you need fear nothing else. He will be your safety.*
Isaiah 8:13-14, TLB

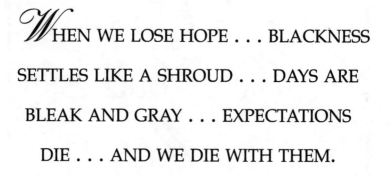

*W*HEN WE LOSE HOPE . . . BLACKNESS
SETTLES LIKE A SHROUD . . . DAYS ARE
BLEAK AND GRAY . . . EXPECTATIONS
DIE . . . AND WE DIE WITH THEM.

WE HAVE NOWHERE TO LOOK . . .

EXCEPT *UP*.

# EIGHTEEN

# *Wounded Tulips*

*T*he dark-haired, attractive mistress of ceremonies startled us by announcing, "The ladies came in early and slit the throat of each tulip."

I glanced at the lovely spring bouquets, containing tulips, daffodils, and iris, that graced each table and the huge arrangement that covered half the grand piano. The blossoms stood tall and proud, including the brilliant tulips, which have a tendency to droop after a few hours in a vase.

She continued, "The growers said that if you slit the throat of each tulip before arranging them, all the energy of the flower goes to healing the wound instead of opening more fully. So the flowers stay fresh-looking and upright longer."

*Incredible*, I thought. But my next thought exclaimed, *Poor tulip!*

I pictured one of those bright red tulips, raised with care and nurtured with tenderness. One day, just as the bud began to open, the tulip was harvested.

"Wonderful," the tulip whispered. "Now I'll be put into a beautiful arrangement to give pleasure to many people."

Then suddenly, the tulip felt a sharp pain as its delicate and slender throat was cut! Wounded, hurt, and bewildered, the flower shuddered.

*I will not let this defeat me*, the tulip thought. And, using its strength to try to repair the wound, the tulip flourished, refusing to die. It didn't realize that its beauty and even its life were being prolonged in the process as it stood straight and tall in the vase. For several days, people enjoyed its beauty.

As I thought about that wounded tulip, this verse pricked my heart: "In faithfulness you [God] have afflicted me" (Psalm 119:75).

*Could it be?* Could it be that one reason God afflicts me is in order for me to remain useful, to stay "beautiful," reflecting His glory for a longer time in my life?

Sometimes He wounds me in loving discipline, but perhaps, at other times, I'm afflicted simply to make me strong. The troubles of my life make me able to stand in the winds of adversity and be less of a hot-house flower.

I cupped my hands around one bright red tulip and looked with awe and compassion at the tiny slit on both sides of its slender throat. I knew God was pleased with His creation of the tulip. May He also be pleased with His creation of me.

*Father, I want to welcome the trials that come into my life as friends, not resent them as intruders, realizing that one reason You allow them is to make me stronger, more able to reflect You.*

Before I was afflicted I went astray,
  but now I obey your word.
You are good, and what you do is good;
  teach me your decrees. (Psalm 119:67-68)

You have forgotten that word of encouragement that addresses you as sons: "My son, do not make light of the Lord's discipline, and do not lose heart when he rebukes you, because the Lord disciplines those he loves, and he punishes everyone he accepts as a son."
  Endure hardship as discipline; God is treating you as sons. (Hebrews 12:5-7)

# NINETEEN

# I Dropped the Football!

*J*ack and I settled on the couch the other night, sharing a bowl of freshly popped corn as we tuned into a mystery drama.

In one scene, Burt Reynolds as B.L. Stryker, the TV private eye, talked with a friend (now a football recruiter for a small university) about their days playing football together.

The scene went something like this:

Friend: "Why do you only tell people about the time you dropped the football in the end zone?"

B.L. (glumly): "Because I *dropped* the ball!"

Friend: "But you made fourteen touchdowns that year. You lead the team in rushing. You sparked the team . . . you. . . ."

B.L. (a low murmur): "Yeeeaah, I guess. . . ."

But you know he is thinking, *But at a critical moment, I dropped the ball!*

The other night I attended a school program. Before a large audience, a third-grade boy forgot a verse he was trying to recite. He tried, forgot, tried again, forgot again, and finally, with prompting, blurted it out.

He took his place with the others on the risers for the final song. But his little face was screwed tight, trying to hold back the tears. He didn't succeed.

My heart ached for him as I thought, *He'll probably remember this night forever as one where he "dropped the ball."*

How often I view my life in such a way.

My piano teacher loved recitals and insisted her students participate in several each year. So I played in a dozen or so in my growing up years.

But I remember only two—during both I started a long two-handed run down the length of the piano keyboard *on the wrong key*. Discordant notes flew like popcorn from an uncovered popper, and the audience, as one, grimaced.

Nobody really cared. They were all parents waiting patiently to hear their own children perform. But, when talk of piano recitals comes up, I tell of those recitals where . . . I dropped the ball!

For every negative expressed, experts say, five positives should be given for reinforcement.

I disagree.

Most of us need ten or twenty or fifty—and even that probably won't do it. We tend to blow out the positives like a sputtering flame while nurturing the negatives with a cupped hand around the candle.

Not so with God. The proud and loving Father sees not the bumbling performance, but looking at our feeblest efforts, smiles in love and . . . applauds.

Can you just see Him smiling and saying to that little boy, "Son, I'm proud of you. I know you tried your best and you wanted to please Me. Well done!"?

I'm sure of it! Sure of it because Gideon won a place in God's hall of fame among the heroes of faith in Hebrews 11. Read Gideon's story in Judges 6–7 and figure *that* one out! Gideon was weak, cowardly, frightened, and made God prove Himself several times before being willing to obey. Yet at their first encounter, we find God calling Gideon a "valiant warrior" (Judges 6:12). Incredible!

God told him to tear down the altar of Baal and Gideon did it at night because he was scared to death! Then, before he would lead the Israelites into battle, he sneaked down to the enemy camp to hear two men relating a dream about their destruction. He needed that to be convinced that God would really deliver Israel. Still, no matter how terrified, Gideon *obeyed*.

God's one expectation and command for us is *obedience.* He knows I'm going to flunk a lot of life's demands, and He has given me advice about that. He tells me not to compare myself with others, to use the gifts that He's given me (not the ones He hasn't given me!), to trust Him for adequacy for the tasks He asks me to do.

When I fall flat on my face and feel like a total failure, I am reminded that my motivation in doing must be to obey God. I am not doing it for people. Knowing God is my director and my audience, makes me attuned to the Father — a Father who cheers me on, who smiles encouragement, who picks me up and dusts me off and washes the dirt from the wounds, who says, "Child, I'm proud of you. You tried. Now forget what lies behind and reach forward to what lies ahead and press toward the goal. You are My beloved."

*Father, please help me put behind me the times I've dropped the ball. You do. Why can't I?*

Brothers, I do not consider myself yet to have taken hold of it. But one thing I do: Forgetting what is behind and straining toward what is ahead, I press on toward the goal to win the prize for which God has called me heavenward in Christ Jesus. (Philippians 3:13-14)

# TWENTY

# *Happy on the Outside*

*T*hey all looked so happy — so together — as they gathered for the women's retreat. They laughed at the jokes of the M.C., applauded loudly for the soloist, sang with gusto as the song leader cheered them on.

But peel away the outside layer and terrible hurts rest just beneath the surface.

"My daughter . . ." her voice broke, then she resumed weakly, "my daughter is a lesbian."

And another, "Last week . . . my former husband shot and killed his girlfriend in front of her children — then turned the gun on himself," she confessed as her eyes filled with tears.

And from a woman with graying hair, "My husband . . . we've been missionaries to South America all our married life. Now our kids are grown, and we're like two strong ships sailing in opposite directions. There's no friendship, no intimacy, no conversation in our marriage."

I listened . . . and my heart reached out silently.

And sometimes — sometimes it seems that it's *all too much.* I feel so inadequate to help, so insufficient in either knowledge or experience. Those women needed encouragement, but what could I say in the face of such raw pain?

It's then that God often says, "Carole, you don't have to say *anything.* Do you think you are the 'mother of comforts'? Child, remember I am the One who comforts. I am the Father of all mercies and the God of all comfort (2 Corinthians 1:3-4). Your job is just to listen . . . and then point them to Me."

So I sighed within myself, took a deep breath, and suggested that as soon as they could, they get some protracted time with the Father and do what Psalm 62:8 tells us to do: "Trust in him [the Lord] at all times, O people [put your name in there]; pour out your hearts to him, for God is our refuge."

When things are too much for me, I go into my room, shut the door, get down on my knees, and pour out my heart—out loud. I start with "A" and go way past "Z," telling the Lord all the details—how I'm feeling, what hurts, how others are involved. I *pour out my heart* as to my very best friend—which He is—only He's better than an earthly friend because He can *do* something about the difficulty and the hurt. And He never reveals secrets!

After I've poured out my heart, I listen . . . listen to His still, small voice speaking. He never fails to give me something—instruction, comfort, ideas, or encouragement. I always get up from my knees with a sense of peace and joy and rest.

I feel so helpless in the face of the horrendous problems that batter down the souls of the people around me. But *God isn't!*

My hope for each of us as God's children is that we learn to pour out our hearts to God!

———————

*Father, thank You that You don't get tired of listening. I would. I do. But You are kind, patient, understanding, and tireless. I feel so blessed to have a Father like You who allows me to pour out my heart—every hurt, care, complaint, trouble—and that You've asked me to! And You listen! You really are a help in time of trouble! Thank You.*

You have filled my heart with greater joy
    than when their grain and new wine abound.

I will lie down and sleep in peace,
 for you alone, O LORD,
 make me dwell in safety. (Psalm 4:7-8)

You hear, O LORD, the desire of the afflicted;
 you encourage them, and you listen to their cry.
  (10:17)

The LORD is my strength and my shield;
 my heart trusts in him, and I am helped.
My heart leaps for joy
 and I will give thanks to him in song. (28:7)

TWENTY-ONE

# *Complaints*

*T*he day began badly and went downhill from there.

Trying to get ready for a five-week trip, my hurry-up speed escalated three gears. Rushing to stuff objects onto a top cupboard shelf, a full bottle of oil-and-vinegar salad dressing fell and shattered on the countertop, splattering its contents over the cabinets, carpeted floor, and my white slacks.

I grabbed some paper towels to sop the goo quickly, and my forehead collided sharply with the corner of the open cabinet door.

Holding my head with one hand while mopping up with the other, I moaned, "This has *not* been a *good* day!"

That was at 8:15 a.m.!

I'm not very objective on a day like that! But sometimes — after — I am able to take a few steps away mentally and listen to myself. And I don't like what I hear. It sounds suspiciously like muttering!

I am so glad that God is eternally patient with me in pointing it out — over and over again. Recently, that happened once more, and it came, as usual, right from God's Word.

I thought Paul's message to the Corinthian church might leave me unaffected this time. After all, he's talking to a pretty sinful bunch of people, and I'm not that bad, right?

After holding up an object lesson for these hardheads

73

about the sinfulness of the children of Israel, Paul gets into specifics. "Do not be idolaters," he intones. (See 1 Corinthians 10:7-19.) My thoughts said, "Check."

"We should not commit sexual immorality," he reminded. And my heart said, "That's so!"

"We should not test the Lord, as some of them did . . ." and I responded, "Right."

But his fourth "never" felled me: "And do not grumble, as some of them did — and were killed by the destroying angel" (verse 10). *Whoops!*

To me, grumbling doesn't seem like such a big deal. Why would God put grumbling alongside idolatry, immorality, and testing Him?

I'm not sure, but He *does*. And as I considered it, I realized that idolatry is *deifying* something other than God, immorality is *defiling* God, testing is *defying* God. And grumbling? Grumbling is *denying* the grace of God. It's saying God isn't treating me right.

I have to confess. Some days I find myself grumbling, complaining, whining, muttering, griping, and groaning.

One day, in that kind of mood, I wrote:

Oh, Lord, I feel like complaining.
> My head hurts,
> my throat's sore,
> wedding plans are escalating,
> it's only two weeks to the big day,
> and now we've had an auto accident!
Not a big one, Lord.
Thank You that no precious one was hurt.
But the hassle!
> To be in the city without our own familiar car,
> driving a friend's tiny substitute . . .
> trying to get the furniture to a house three hours
> away
> when the trailer hitch is on the banged-up vehicle!
And Jack is several states away!
I feel so unable to cope.
But just now I read Your Word,

"Cast all your anxiety on him
because he cares for you" (1 Peter 5:7).
You care!
You not only *can* cope but You are willing to cope!

*Father, help me to take the heaped-up concerns of my heart
and dump them on You. Because You've told me You want
them . . . and me!*
*You are wonderful. Thank You.*
*P.S. Lord, and forgive me . . . forgive me for complaining!*

Cast your cares on the LORD
and he will sustain you;
he will never let the righteous fall. (Psalm 55:22)

## TWENTY-TWO
# *Pain*

---

*I*t's April 1979. I am waiting for my sister to die.

I stare at those words now and shiver. I die a little inside at the thoughts I am thinking.

I sit in her hospital room by her bed. The hard, straight chair makes me stay awake through the long hours. She moans, cries for a shot to relieve her pain, vomits. Her skin is gray, her hands the color of the white sheet they limply rest against.

I remember her as a little girl of five in a white rabbit coat with skinny white leggings. How she loved that coat and how she hated those leggings. We, her older brother and sister, didn't help by saying she looked like a marshmallow on two sticks! She wept — and I weep at the memory of our cruel words.

We became friends when she was a junior in a Christian academy — I was a junior at college nearby. We stood up for each other as we married.

I reflect on the humiliation of dying. The humiliation of a meticulous person drooling from the corner of her mouth due to paralysis of her face from pressure on the brain. The humiliation of becoming bald for one whose hair had been truly her crown of beauty. The humiliation of having to depend on other hands — sometimes not-so-willing hands — to cut meat, to feed her even a soft-boiled egg. The humiliation of being exposed and poked and tested by unknown hands. The humiliation of having a student nurse see a picture of a just-married daughter taped to a hospital closet and asking, "Is this your granddaughter?" They had been taken for sisters such a short time before.

And weakness. . . . The weakness of being unable to wipe away a tear or guide a glass of water to a mouth. The weakness of being unable to remember and yet be aware of not remembering.

I break down hearing my husband's dear sympathetic voice over the phone 1,000 miles away. I cry when the pastor pats my arm. I have to go into another room to weep when my sister prays—for her husband, for me. She prays for strength for *us*—she who has no strength. She prays for grace for us to face what is ahead. She prays to die gently, and I pray with her.

But I cry.

The gray, misty day reflects my spirit. Yet it is spring. Dirty heaps of snow are losing their battle for existence. Underneath, the crocus's valiant shoot will eventually win. I am glad for the visual reminder. I reflect on the song, "Good news! Children of God never die!"

But my emotions run the black gamut from despair and anger over my sister's suffering to rejoicing in the sure hope of eternity. I feel weak and trembly from the struggle and ambivalence of my own emotions. I weep inside, but fight to stay calm in the face of her suffering.

I decide to read in my Bible where I last left off, but three chapters of doom in Israel do nothing to lift my heart. Then suddenly there it is!

> He will swallow up death forever.
> The Sovereign LORD will wipe away the tears
> from all faces. . . .
> The LORD has spoken. (Isaiah 25:8)

I look at my sister's dear face. I remember the words of a friend, "We are not in the land of the living going to the land of the dying. We are in the land of the dying going to the land of the living."

I think, *One day . . . not too far distant . . . those who believe will all be there . . . in the land of the living!*

We will cry no more. *For the Lord has spoken.*

And I whisper softly, "Hallelujah!" For I know that *it is so.*

*Father God, thank You that I can know without a doubt that the people I have loved in this life, those who know You, are with You after death and that all of their pain has ended. Help me to look forward to the day when You will wipe away all my pain.*

The body that is sown is perishable, it is raised imperishable; it is sown in dishonor, it is raised in glory; it is sown in weakness it is raised in power; it is sown a natural body, it is raised a spiritual body. (1 Corinthians 15:42-44

Then I heard what sounded like a great multitude, like the roar of rushing waters and like loud peals of thunder, shouting:
"Hallelujah!
For our Lord God Almighty reigns.
Let us rejoice and be glad
and give him glory!
For the wedding of the Lamb has come,
and his bride has made herself ready.
Fine linen, bright and clean,
was given her to wear."
(Fine linen stands for the righteous acts of the saints.)
(Revelation 19:6-8)

PART FIVE

## He Triumphs In Praise

*Praise the* LORD. . . .
*Praise him for his acts of power;*
*praise him for his surpassing greatness. . . .*
*Let everything that has*
*breath praise the* LORD.
*Praise the* LORD.

PSALM 150:1,2,6

---·❦·---

IF, AS I'VE READ, "JOY IS THE FLAG

FLOWN FROM THE CASTLE WHEN THE

KING IS IN RESIDENCE," THEN PRAISE

MUST BE THE KING'S MIGHTY

MARCHING BAND PLAYING

IN HIS COURTYARD.

# TWENTY-THREE

# *Weddings*

———➤•◀———

he candle lighters—the mothers of the bride and of the groom—were having trouble. Try as they might, the candles would not stay lit. After failing on several attempts, they had no choice but to leave four of the fourteen candles dark and sheepishly walk back down the aisle.

I've always said that if at least one thing doesn't go wrong at a wedding, a couple probably isn't really married. But some weddings are total disasters.

Picture the wedding where the flower girl inadvertently stood on the bride's train. When the bride turned to say her vows, her dress ripped halfway off around the waist. She finished the ceremony holding her dress up with one hand.

Visualize the flower girl who found the wedding dress hanging in the bedroom before the ceremony and, deciding it was too long, solved that problem by shortening it with shears.

Perhaps the most shocking story I've heard was about the wedding that began late. When the bride finally came down the aisle, the minister asked, "Do you take this man to be your lawfully wedded husband?" and firmly the bride replied, "No, I will not."

Thinking she had misunderstood, the minister repeated the question, and again the bride responded, "No, I will not."

The confused minister asked the bride and groom to step

into the anteroom, and as they did so, he inquired what was going on. The bride explained, "I was unavoidably detained coming to the wedding and when I arrived, he . . ." — she nodded toward the groom — "he cursed me. I realized as I was walking down the aisle that I could not marry any man who would curse me on my wedding day."

One recent catastrophe I heard about concerned a bridal party that arrived at a local military chapel at 9:45 a.m. for changing and picture taking before a scheduled 11:00 a.m. wedding, only to find the door of the chapel locked. Frantic searching did not turn up the officer of the day — the only one who had a key. The flowers arrived, followed by the minister, and soon the guests, but the chapel remained firmly bolted. At long last, the officer of the day came — at 12:00 p.m. in order to open the chapel for a 1:00 p.m. wedding! The bride had to dress in an open-air foyer. The wedding took place in fifteen minutes (the minister had to be across town for a 1:00 p.m. wedding, and the next wedding party was waiting). And only half the guests stayed for the luncheon reception, which finally got under way at 2:00 p.m. And to add to the calamity, the wedding pictures came back blurred and discolored.

At Jack's and my wedding, the best man lost my ring (found an hour later between the cushions of a couch), and Jack caused me a fit of giggles as he murmured, "With this wing I thee wed."

⁕

Years ago in a small village in a country where there were no grocery stores and where most water wasn't fit to drink, a wedding took place. The ceremony itself went smoothly, but misfortune struck the reception. A servant looked into the cupboard and his face went white. Frantically, he searched the cool cellar, but to no avail. There was no more wine to serve the guests and no place to buy or borrow any more, either. (See John 2:1-11.)

Mary, somehow aware of the situation, turned to her son and asked Him to do something. Moments later the servants were pouring rich, red wine from pots which a moment before held water.

When the wine was served to the one in charge of the banquet, he pulled the groom aside and puzzled, "Everyone brings out the choice wine first and then the cheaper wine after the guests have had too much to drink; but you have saved the best till now."

For His first miracle, Jesus turned disaster to delight.

I stand amazed, astonished at the Lord's concern both for His mother's request and for the success of the wedding. I am astounded not just that Jesus turned the water into wine, but at the *quality* of that wine.

I am also overwhelmed by the astonishing obedience of those servants. Have you ever wondered about them? We have no record of *when* the water turned to wine, but for some reason I think it still looked like water when the servants were told to pour it into the glasses of the guests. What if, looking at water, the servants had refused to serve it? The faith and obedience of those servants could be a big part of this incredible story!

At any rate, I'm glad that Christ's first miracle was performed at a wedding. It demonstrates — to me at least — His thoughtfulness and care in a situation that wasn't life-threatening or dangerous, but simply one that could have proved embarrassing. He reached out in His love, not to raise the dead but to give joy to the living, not to give sight to the blind but to alleviate discouragement, not to provide for profound need but to fulfill a desperate want. In doing so, Christ demonstrated to the world His concern for the totality of our lives.

Long years ago, God taught me a bit concerning His interest in the details of my life. Oh, yes, He's there in power for the giants in my life, but He is also there — with love — for the "dailies." He walks through the details of each day with me and shows His care and concern — not only for the wedding but for the minutes and hours and years that follow the wedding as well. He has promised to meet my *needs*, but my small everyday wants are part of His concern too.

And often when I reach out to Him and whisper, "Please

. . . do something," I am awed and amazed by His involvement in the everyday details of my very ordinary life.

*Lord Jesus, thank You for the care You've shown, both to others and to me, in the typical moments I face each day. Help me focus on You and Your ability to act even when my dilemma seems trivial.*

How precious to me are your thoughts, O God!
How vast is the sum of them!
Were I to count them,
    they would outnumber the grains of sand.
    (Psalm 139:17-18)

# TWENTY-FOUR

# *Thanks, Mom!*

his year, Mom Mayhall turned an active ninety-four, and I have to tell you, she's incredible!

Twice a year she flies to Colorado for a visit, and every time she enters an airplane, she asks to see the pilots. Then she says, "Hi. I'm Ruth, and I'd like to pray for you and the safety of this airplane." She's never been refused.

When she entered the cockpit this last time in July, the pilot said, "Well, hi, Ruth. You've prayed with me before!"

Before taking off, an attendant knelt by her seat and said quietly, "Ruth, your prayers have saved this airplane. We just had a near miss on the runway and all of the crew is shaking. Thanks for praying!" An airline employee in another city brought a wheelchair to help Mom make her connection and said, "Oh, you're Ruth. You're the one who prayed and saved the airplane." The word had obviously gotten around!

Like I said, she's incredible! She's also a challenge to me.

I've made the remark often that at my age I don't look *outside* like I feel *inside*. That sometimes I catch my reflection in a store window and think, *Who's* that? And sometimes, I focus on what I don't like about getting older.

I've never heard my mother-in-law do that! And I got to thinking this morning about the reasons *why* she doesn't.

She really *does* have her eyes fixed—not on the temporary but on the eternal, not on the "momentary" but on the forever.

In June she was ninety-four, but in her spirit, she is *young*.
I've been thinking a lot about that too, this morning.
So often, I get my focus wrong.

I'm inclined to look at the wrinkles, the increasing gray in my hair, the way I think people see me, my energy being more quickly consumed, the things I can no longer do.

But that's *wrong*—at least it's wrong to *focus* on those things.

Second Corinthians 4:16-18 says, "Therefore we do not lose heart. Though outwardly we are wasting away, yet inwardly we are being renewed day by day. For our light and momentary troubles are achieving for us an eternal glory that far outweighs them all. So we fix our eyes not on what is seen, but on what is unseen. For what is seen is temporary, but what is unseen is eternal."

I need to concentrate on realizing that as I get older, I have lived more days of "being renewed" inside. Therefore the inside of me is more "youthful," stronger, fresher.

I have experienced more of life and have a clear perspective on Heaven and its glories. I can visualize that no matter what I go through, it is a light and momentary affliction in the light of eternity! Those very troubles are achieving for me eternal glory that far outweighs them all!

So! I am to fix my eyes not on what is seen (getting older)—the temporary—but on what is unseen—the eternal (getting a new body and living forever with the Lord!).

Oh, I want to get that so fixed in my mind (as with the super epoxy glue) that I'd live it every moment! Then I'd have my emphasis right.

Second Corinthians 5:1 says that my earthly tent (what a picture of something temporary) will someday be destroyed and will be upgraded (and what an upgrade!) to a building (permanent!) from God—an eternal house in Heaven not built with human hands but *built by God!*

Does that mean I'm always up? No. Verse 2 says, "Meanwhile we groan" (that's natural!) and "are burdened" (verse 4) because we want to be clothed with a heavenly dwelling.

The exciting thing is that God "has made us for this very

purpose" (verse 5)! And the result should be that "we make it our goal to please him" (verse 9).

Mom figured this out long ago. I hope I learn it soon!

---

*Father, help me not to be so occupied with the negatives of this "wasting away" process. I really do want to have my heart fixed on what is eternal.*

"No eye has seen,
      no ear has heard,
no mind has conceived
      what God has prepared for those who love him" —
but God has revealed it to us by his Spirit.
(1 Corinthians 2:9-10)

# TWENTY-FIVE

# *Winning . . . Long Term*

*T*he small plaque caught my attention. You've seen the one. It says, "Lord, give me patience. And do it RIGHT NOW."

I grin, then I grimace, feeling as though someone peeked into my nature.

I find myself little different than the impatient "instant" world around me. Our world wants it—and often *has* it—now. Instant credit cards, instant meals, instant entertainment.

But as I reflect, I don't see "instant" as one of God's goals. Long-term gains, in God's economy, beat instant every time.

Just consider Hebrews 11:13-14, about some of the heroes of faith: "All these people were still living by faith when they died. They did not receive the things promised; they only saw them and welcomed them from a distance. And they admitted that they were aliens and strangers on earth."

We'd never put up with that today! Not receiving the promise? Horrors. Seeing things from a distance? Never! Welcoming them? Hysterical!

The examples God gives us of biblical heroes—Abel, Enoch, Noah, Abraham—looked at things in a way we seldom do. Of course they wanted to see God's promises fulfilled quickly, but somehow they also kept firmly in mind the "long-term" aspect of the promises as well.

The fulfillment of the short-term promises encouraged

them: Abel's sacrifice was accepted; Enoch was translated to Heaven; Noah survived the flood and experienced rebuilding the land; Abraham had Isaac and lived to see him reproduce.

But the stability of their lives was firmly secured by their future focus, their eternal perspective. They were *still living by faith* (in the long-term promises) when they died.

I'm grateful that God usually doesn't make me wait too long to experience what He says He will do. I'm sure He is aware of my impatience! But I am thinking more these days of promises for the future, which are *so much bigger*!

---

Her face held a sweetness — almost a radiance — as she told our small group, "I'm having open heart surgery next Wednesday. If the operation is a success, I'll be free of the shortness of breath and have the energy I used to have. If it isn't" — a bit of God's glory was in her smile — "if it isn't, I'll be with Jesus." She hesitated, then added softly, "Either way *I win.*"

We remembered her words with comfort a week later when our dear friend, Carol, entered the gates of Heaven.

She won. Long term.

---

God continually lifts my sights to eternity. Life is most discouraging and frustrating if our focus is on the now instead of the "then."

God gave us only one child. I longed for more. Cried for more. Begged for more. But Lynn was to be it.

I thought I heard God saying He would give me more children. Was I taking it as a "short-term" promise of natural children when He was giving me a "long-term" promise of spiritual children multiplied?

I longed to be an overseas missionary — to me, the highest calling of all. Several times in our lives that seemed eminent, but the door closed firmly every time. Was I looking for short-term fulfillment when the Lord was preparing ones

I could touch at home who would go to the ends of the earth—including my daughter? Was I looking at "now" when the Lord was saying "then"?

Whenever I can't see immediate results of what I do, I tend to think of it as failure. Yet Hebrews says that Abel "still speaks" though he is dead. The effect of a life can live on long after the body is put into the ground. If I am obeying God day by day, results must be left to Him for what He leads me to do. And maybe after I'm dead He will use me to "still speak." That's both a comfort and an awesome promise . . . long term!

I need balance and wisdom between the here and now and the forever future, between praying for the fulfillment of short-term promises and keeping my heart, thoughts, and desires rooted in God's long-term promises.

Here I see the short term only. But when the long-term promises are a reality instead of a hope, I'm confident that the short-term ones, which give my life joy now, will fade into *insignificance.*

———◆◆———

*Lord, a line from an old hymn is playing over and over in my heart: "What a foretaste of glory divine!" Whatever joys and beauty my life holds in the present, it is merely a fore-taste. May I paraphrase Romans 8:18 this way, "I consider my present sufferings . . . and my present home, joys, adven-tures, loves . . . not worth comparing with the glory that will be revealed in us—and to us as well."*

*Lord, I want to set my eyes on Heaven . . . on You, being grateful for the way You reveal Yourself to me in the short term, but always conscious of all that You have for me long term . . . in my forever.*

> Your kingdom is an everlasting kingdom,
> and your dominion endures through all generations.
> The LORD is faithful to all his promises
> and loving toward all he has made. (Psalm 145:13)

# TWENTY-SIX

# *Welcome*

---

*S*he was, maybe, two and a half. She stood peering down the jetway, an intense look on her face and a small bunch of wildflowers glued in her fist. Diminutive jeans. Stocking feet, no shoes.

Her mother, hugging a smaller child to her chest, stood behind her. I wondered if I'd recognize the one they were waiting for so eagerly.

Bored business travelers deplaned. Families. Aged women. As each person exited, I mentally crossed off the possibility.

By this time, most people had left the jetway, and the child's face screwed up with worry. "Where is he, Mommy? Is he coming?"

Her mother nodded in assurance.

Then, smiles. "There he is!" the mother exclaimed, glimpsing him above the heads of the stragglers.

I could have guessed by *his* face—eyes crinkled, huge smile. The lettered A cap carelessly sitting on his head, Madras shorts, crumpled T-shirt, running shoes—all went unnoticed by the welcoming committee.

*This* man was greeted with such joy and ceremony, it was as though the world stopped a minute to watch. He knelt to the height of his small daughter and gathered her in his arms. Then, standing up, he encircled his wife and baby and gave each a resounding kiss.

I watched the small ceremony with a tug on my heart and a smile.

The same evening, stepping off my own flight, another tableau. A father this time and two small children. Between them a hand-lettered cardboard sign, which read:

WELCOME HOME, MOMMY

Someday . . .

Someday I will be greeted like that.

Eagerly.

I will hear the words from One who loves me beyond my comprehension. He will say, *"Welcome home! Welcome home, My beloved daughter!"*

Tell me, isn't that worth waiting for?

*Father, what a joy it is going to be when You welcome me home. Help me not to focus on the passing years but to be filled with anticipation day by day of the joy of reunion— with my loved ones who have gone before, but most of all with You.*

I heard a loud voice from the throne saying, "Now the dwelling of God is with men, and he will live with them. They will be his people, and God himself will be with them and be their God. He will wipe every tear from their eyes. There will be no more death or mourning or crying or pain, for the old order of things has passed away." (Revelation 21:3-4)

# TWENTY-SEVEN

# *Overflowing with Gratitude*

*I*f . . . in some magical way . . . I could run my life backward and take a video of this past month, then process it through a computer which could discern the true attitude of my heart, and finally display only those moments in which my heart was truly joyful—when it was "overflowing with thanksgiving"—then, with that same magic, the film could be shown this very minute. . . .

I wonder. How much time would it take to play?

Would there be any moments at all to see? Or would—devastating thought—only a blank screen show?

The Bible says I am to walk in Christ in a way that is "overflowing with thanksgiving" (Colossians 2:7)—a condition of heart that is not optional. But that isn't easy!

Recently, I read Colossians 1:9-12, which says:

> We have not stopped . . . asking God to fill you with the knowledge of his will through all spiritual wisdom and understanding. And we pray this in order that you may live a life worthy of the Lord and may please him in every way: bearing fruit in every good work, growing in the knowledge of God, being strengthened with all power according to his glorious might so that you may have great endurance and patience, and joyfully giving thanks to the Father.

In a particularly frustrating situation I was going through, I knew God's ultimate goal for me was that I be "steadfast and patient." So I tried. And I found myself being patient by gritting my teeth. Patient by keeping contact with the irritating person as brief as possible. Patient by boiling over only in my thoughts.

Then I took another look at these verses and winced! Because, according to this passage, *that isn't enough!* The next words add "joyfully giving thanks to the Father."

I was to be patient with *joy*. Steadfast with *thanksgiving*, ruling out my "martyred" attitude.

How in the world is that possible?

I read it again and shook my head. I had been reading "growing in the knowledge of God . . . so that you may have great endurance and patience," and I had been mentally leaving out a critical phrase right in the middle: "being strengthened with all power according to his glorious might."

*Only* as I am strengthened by His might can I be patient — not my strength, but His power is essential for patience with *joy*.

It starts with prayer. Then as I grow in the knowledge of God, as I am strengthened by His glorious might, I *will* have the ability to be patient . . . and endure — with *joy* and *thanksgiving*.

* * *

*Lord, help me not to be content just to be patient. Just to endure. I want my patience and my endurance to be overflowing with thanksgiving. May it be full of joy. Thank You that You are able to do this in me.*

The LORD will surely comfort . . .
    and will look with compassion. . . .
Joy and gladness will be found in her,
    thanksgiving and the sound of singing. (Isaiah 51:3)

# TWENTY-EIGHT

# *Delight in the Lord*

*T*he Christmas season bordered on disaster. It wasn't the jammed-full-of-people house. It wasn't that for fourteen days from attic to basement our home looked as though a cyclone had hit and tarried. It wasn't the violent version of the twenty-four-hour stomach flu that made the rounds impartially among our relatives. It wasn't even the fractured plans and the confusion of last-minute changes.

There had been some unintentional hurts and disappointments, and it grieved us to see loved ones downcast, but it was far more even than that.

Where was my *joy*? If, in the midst of troubled circumstances, God's joy was absent, something was wrong! I knew that. However, the exact nature of my problem eluded me.

"I have to confess, Lord. I'm confused. I'm certainly not living above the circumstances," I admitted one morning.

So I began a Bible study on "delight," and a verse I'd memorized long ago stopped me cold! "Delight thyself in the Lord" (Psalm 37:4, KJV).

I guess I thought that delight would come from the joys of the Christmas season, seeing beloved family and friends. And of course, that is often true in part. But God is saying something far deeper here. I am to delight myself in the *Lord*. And more. I am to delight *myself* in the Lord!

So I whispered to Him, "*How* do I do that?"

Suddenly I was reminded of a phrase that had played

constantly in my head those two weeks: "I don't mind the physical work of multiple meals, making plans for entertaining, cleaning, etc. What really gets to me is when people aren't happy despite all my effort." I nodded to myself, thinking how true that was.

Then another thought made me blink. "It *is* true. But is it *right*?"

It dawned on me then that I had been assuming the overwhelming responsibility of trying to ensure that everyone was "delighted"—a responsibility that was not only far too big for me, but one God never intended me to have! I was responsible only to delight *myself*, and the only One I can or should delight *in* is the Lord.

Each person had the personal responsibility to do the same.

"But, Lord," I argued, "I'm still confused! You've said to weep with those who weep—that we are to bear one another's burdens. Could I ever—would You ever want me to—be unaffected by the feelings and concerns of those around me?"

"Of course not, child. I want your heart always to be tender toward the feelings of others. But that can't be your primary focus. Even the feelings of others mustn't be allowed to rob you of My joy."

I whispered, "My eyes have been pulled away from You—haven't they, Lord? I guess in my humanness, there will always be times when I focus on problems instead of on the Problem-solver.

"But Lord, please enable me to have shorter and shorter lapse time!"

---

When anxiety was great within me,
　　your consolation brought joy to my soul.
　　　(Psalm 94:19)

# TWENTY-NINE

# A Sense of Wonder

H e was bundled up in a padded blue snowsuit so completely that only his face was left uncovered. He stood, face uplifted, as the big snowflakes drifted lazily down. He blinked as one touched his eyelashes. Laughing with delight, he stuck out his tongue as far as it would go, waited until it caught a huge flake, and grinned as it melted. His mouth formed an O as he clapped his hands together in astonished delight.

His first snowfall, and he was . . . *filled with wonder.*

---

What makes a person old at twenty and keeps another young at eighty?

I think it is that *sense of wonder* — the insatiable curiosity and delight concerning God, the world, and people.

Solomon, for all his wisdom, was jaded. When I read the book of Ecclesiastes, I see that he had *too much* of everything. Too much wisdom. Too much wealth. Too many women. Life to him was a wearisome, meaningless mess. The way he saw it, the sun came up and went down; the oceans never filled up; the wind kept blowing; generations came and went; what had been done would be done again. The whole thing was boring and tedious!

There was no wonder left for Solomon . . . no curiosity in

how the earth turned on its axis or where the wind came from, no awe in who put it there or astonishment in the infinite variety of such things as sea shells, snowflakes, and faces of human beings.

For the wisest man on earth, Solomon was kind of dumb! He knew great truth: God makes everything beautiful in its time. God has set eternity in the hearts of men. Satisfaction is a gift from God. And whatever God does will endure forever. (See Ecclesiastes 3:11,13-14.)

In Ecclesiastes 5:19-20, Solomon even states the key to *joy* and *contentment*: "Moreover, when God gives any man wealth and possessions, and enables him to enjoy them, to accept his lot and be happy in his work — this is a gift of God. He seldom reflects on the days of his life, because God keeps him occupied with gladness of heart."

But apparently *knowing* that and *experiencing* it were two different things for Solomon. Knowing the key to joy, he lived most of his life feeling depressed, weary, and futile, without goals or satisfaction.

When I think about it, Solomon isn't so different from many of us *most* of the time!

We Christ-ones *know* the keys to having a glad heart. They are spelled out for us clearly:

First, enjoy what we have (enabled by God) as we accept our "lot" — which means accepting whatever "portion and cup" (Psalm 16:5) God has given. If we do that we won't feel guilty if we "have" or cheated if we "have not."

Second, be happy in our work, knowing that God has and is directing our steps and there is *purpose* in our days.

Third, don't dwell in the past — live in the present with each moment being lived "to the hilt" and let *God* keep us occupied with *gladness* of heart.

God gives us the key to contentment and joy, but He didn't say it would be easy! It takes growing in spiritual maturity, in goals, in interest of what He has for us. It means *occupying* our hearts with Him.

But, with the Lord's help, it *is* possible.

So, hey!

Examine a dandelion. Play tag with a child. Stick out

your tongue and taste a snowflake!
    And *never* lose your *sense of wonder*!

*Lord, help me to approach each day with a sense of being mentally on tiptoe in expectation for what is around the corner. I never want to lose the delight of satisfaction in "the now" nor the anticipation for what is ahead. May I . . . accept my portion and my cup knowing they are from You. Help me to take joy in my work knowing You are directing my days. May I live each moment to the fullest with Your gladness of heart and drink from Your river of delights. And Father, help me never . . . ever . . . to lose my sense of wonder.*

Though you have not seen him, you love him; and even though you do not see him now, you believe in him and are filled with an inexpressible and glorious joy. (1 Peter 1:8)

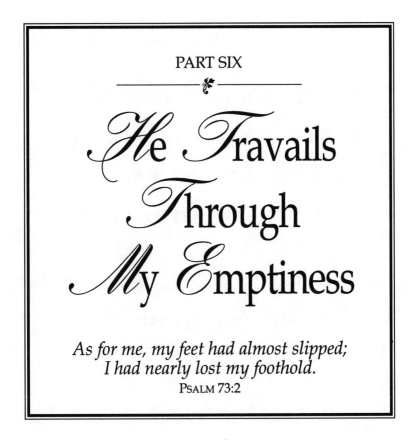

PART SIX

# He Travails Through My Emptiness

*As for me, my feet had almost slipped;*
*I had nearly lost my foothold.*
PSALM 73:2

---※---

*E*MPTY: CONTAINING NOTHING;

HAVING NO WORTH OR PURPOSE;

USELESS AND UNSATISFYING;

WITHOUT MEANING OR FORCE.

FATHER, *THAT'S EXACTLY HOW I FEEL!*

HELP ME, PLEASE!

# THIRTY

# *Sincere – But Wrong*

*I* was anxious. Three reserved places at our table for ten remained empty. Small Victorian paper cornucopias filled with candy had been placed at each setting, salads set on the table, the meal paid for in advance, but the three guests didn't arrive. Lynn waited in the foyer of the Christmas-decorated Air Force officer's club in vain. She was concerned whether the falling snow and icy roads had caused an accident for her coworker and the worker's mother and grandmother.

The luncheon program progressed as we kept an eye on the door. The carolers in long dresses sang of Christmas bells. A delicious lunch was served. The speaker talked of not letting the glitter of the season obstruct Christ's glory in our lives.

But the chairs remained empty.

As soon as she could, Lynn telephoned her friend. What had happened? Was she all right?

In an absolutely devastated voice, Lynn's friend said that, yes, they'd started out even though it was snowing heavily. They'd arrived promptly at 11:00 a.m., hung up their coats and tried in vain to find the room where the luncheon was being held. Then they went out to the car and got the luncheon invitation, which had the name of the facility and the map on it. It was only then they realized their mistake. They had gone miles north of town to a different Air Force base, while the luncheon was being held south of town — probably thirty miles away. They were devastated! Lynn's friend was a recent Christian, didn't have a good relationship with her mom, and wanted this to be a time for her mom to hear about the love of God and hopefully mend some hurts in their relationship. All of them had looked at the invitation — they'd even been reading the map to get there!

Sincere — but wrong. And all the sorrow in the world couldn't change the results.

I thought of this verse in Proverbs: "There is a way that seems right to a man, but in the end it leads to death" (14:12). And I wondered. Of all the people who were rushing around the malls that Christmas, how many were making the same mistake? Were they, perhaps sincerely, trying to make sense of the season, trying to put joy back in their Christmas, trying to see past the glitter to the glory? But were they sincerely trying to do it without Christ in them — the One who *is* the hope of glory?

Sincere — but wrong.

Our friends missed only a lunch.

But frantic, frenzied people, in their search for meaning and purpose in life, may very well miss . . . *God.*

———

*Father, I'm grateful that I haven't missed Your salvation. But I wonder what I may have missed that You wanted to give me. Peace, perhaps? Joy? Gentleness?*

*Have I sincerely pursued a course only to find that it leads to nothing? Have I missed the mark?*

*May Your gentle Spirit guard the course of my life toward the final purpose of gaining all You mean for me to have . . . for all eternity.*

"Enter through the narrow gate. For wide is the gate and broad is the road that leads to destruction, and many enter through it. But small is the gate and narrow the road that leads to life, and only a few find it." (Matthew 7:13-14)

# THIRTY-ONE

# *Filling the Emptiness*

I stopped long enough that day to take a hard look deep inside of me. I wasn't shocked to see *nothing there*.

I'd been going on my reserve tank for some time and had depleted all resources. The problem was, I couldn't stop! A zillion things still needed to be done for a major trip a few days away, and somehow I'd scheduled a retreat the weekend before. So there I was—rebelling inwardly at being hundreds of miles from home, needing to give what I didn't have.

It was then God led me to Psalm 51:10, which says, "Create in me a pure heart," and stopped me at that first phrase. His voice spoke to my heart with clarity and encouragement, and I wrote:

Create in me, Lord . . .
    a pure heart, yes.
    But Father, even more.
Create in me . . .
    (out of nothing for that's what *creation* means)
    an expectant heart. . . .
May I stand on tiptoe
    waiting each moment in joyous anticipation
    for what *You* are going to do!
Create in me an enthusiastic heart—
    "en theo"—meaning "in God," God in me,
    filled to overflowing with You, Lord!

Create in me a laughing heart—
    one that sees the serendipities of an autumn leaf
    and mist upon the mountains
    and hears the chuckle of a child.
Create in me a heart of integrity—
    to be *real*,
    not to talk above my walk,
    not to try to *impress*.
Create in me a caring heart—
    tender toward the hurts and happenings of others,
    more concerned with their needs than with my own.
Create in me an attentive heart—
    able to hear Your whisper,
    and moment by moment listen to Your voice.
Create in me a contented heart—
    at peace with the circumstances of life.
Create in me a hungry heart—
    longing to love You more,
    desiring Your Word,
    reaching . . . stretching . . . for more of You.
Creator Lord, *create in me*. Amen.

And you know . . . *He did.*

---

*Father, besides the freshness of Your new creation of all sorts of things in me, I need to be renewed and restored and to have a willing spirit . . . this day and every day.*

    Create in me a pure heart, O God,
        and renew a steadfast spirit within me. . . .
    Restore to me the joy of your salvation
        and grant me a willing spirit, to sustain me.
           (Psalm 51:10,12)

# THIRTY-TWO

# *Not a Good Day*

*E*ric, age five, looked up at me, eyes brimming with tears, lips trembling.

"Eric, what's the matter?" I asked.

He responded, "This has not been a good day for me."

"What hasn't been good, honey?"

"Well," he answered tearfully, "Grampa was too busy to show me how to throw a boomerang, no one will play Uno with me, I don't have anything to do. It just hasn't been a good day for me."

I shook my head. He had unwrapped and played with an early Christmas present, been taken to the park, had a mountain of toys available to him. But because of two immediate disappointments, it "hadn't been a good day for him."

I thought, *Lord, how like me!*

I ought to know better.

Eric is five.

I am a grandmother.

---

*Lord, You surround me with beauty, give me health and strength, blessings without number. But then a couple of disappointments come along and I say to You, "This hasn't been a good day for me." Forgive me, Lord.*

Therefore the LORD longs to be gracious to you,
And therefore He waits on high to have compassion
   on you.
For the LORD is a God of justice;
How blessed are all those who long for Him.
   (Isaiah 30:18, NASB)

# THIRTY-THREE

# I Can't Even See Me!

he wails of her young son wakened the mother in the middle of the night. Rushing to his room, she snapped on the hall light, but found her son huddled with the covers over his head. His night light had burned out.

"What's the matter, Russie?" she questioned anxiously.

"Mommy," he cried, "it's so dark in here, I can't even see *me!*"

I both sympathized and identified with that small boy. Russie didn't know that all he had to do was throw back the covers and let the light in. While I've discovered that God teaches me the deepest lessons in the darkest times, I've also learned that He wants me to get rid of the hindrances and allow His light to shine on the situation. The light dispels darkness and encourages my heart.

King David had every reason to be discouraged—after all, his village had been destroyed and burned, his family and people taken captive, and his men were talking of stoning him. In those dark times, he "encouraged himself in the Lord his God" (1 Samuel 30:6, KJV).

But how do I "encourage myself"?

Let me name two ways.

*Prayer does it!* The other day I was praying about this whole matter of getting older, and I heard myself saying to the Lord, "Father, I don't want to peter out . . . nor do I want to putter out. But what I want is. . . ." I hesitated. How *do* I want to finish the course of life? And then into my heart came the words of Philippians 3:14 — "I press on toward the goal to win the prize for which God has called me heavenward in Christ Jesus."

That was it! So I finished my prayer, "Father, I don't want to peter out or putter out of life. Instead I want to *press on* to take hold of that for which Christ Jesus took hold of me and press on toward the goal You have for me."

An encouragement to my heart? You bet! A joy to my soul? Definitely!

*God's Word does it!* Almost every page contains verses of great encouragement to me. And through it, He continually renews my heart.

Every time I read the story of Christ calming the sea in Mark 4:35-41, I've been puzzled with the phrase, "There were also other boats with him." Why would Mark, led by the Spirit of God, include that bit of information?

Recently a couple of ideas came into my mind as I read that splendid story once again.

Christ had been preaching to a multitude of people that day and when evening came, He said to His disciples, "Let us go over to the other side." So, apparently without stopping to get any provisions, such as a change of clothes or a toothbrush, they "took him along, just as he was."

Perhaps some people had come by sea to hear Jesus, or maybe fishermen lived on the shore where He spoke. In any case, when they saw Him leave, they — probably impetuously — hopped into their boats and followed Him.

Suddenly a furious storm hit, and their boats were inundated, filling up, going under. But Jesus was someplace else — in *another* boat. They could no longer see Him through the torrents of water. They could no longer hear Him for the raging of the sea. They found themselves cut off. Alone.

Have you ever been completely in the dark, feeling like the people in one of those "other boats"? I have. There have been times when Christ didn't seem even to *be* in the boat of my life, let alone in control.

But you know, when Christ said to the raging sea, "Quiet! Be still!" the water calmed not just for the people in His boat who could see Him but for all the "other boats" as well. He saved them all! And suddenly the people in those boats could see Him. Could hear Him. Were awed by Him.

And, I suspect, they knew then that He had been there all the time!

Of course, if Christ is our Lord, we are never *really* alone. He is always with us, and the moment we yell "Help!" we will be aware of that. The lights will come on. The storm will calm.

So when we feel deserted, alone, or abandoned, our feelings lie! For me, encouragement comes in knowing that He will save me from the fury of the storm whether or not I feel His presence—whether or not I can see or hear Him—just as He saved all the people, even those in the other boats. That's the kind of Savior we have!

So how do I encourage myself when things seem dark? Talking with and listening to God helps me every time.

*Father, I want to learn Your lessons well. If that means remaining in the dark, help me to trust You when I cannot see. But when encouragement is only a yell away, may I learn to "encourage myself" as David did.*

*Remind me of Your words . . .*

I have set the LORD always before me.
    Because he is at my right hand,
    I will not be shaken.
Therefore my heart is glad and my tongue rejoices;
    my body also will rest secure. (Psalm 16:8-9)

# THIRTY-FOUR

# *Never Alone*

*I*'d never gone anywhere alone like that before. But the day was gorgeous, Jack was in meetings, and I was the only one around.

So I gathered my courage in my bag, talked it over with the Lord, and headed the eleven miles south (big deal!) in our rented car to Marineland, Florida.

As I bought my ticket—rejoicing in the 10 percent off for AAA members—I glanced around at the groups, couples, and families sauntering in.

*Mmmmm,* I thought. *I must be the only person this Saturday to come to an amusement park alone.*

But I didn't *feel* alone that bright February day. Now, I admit to being a "people person" who enjoys sharing the joys of special experiences, but I'd asked the Lord to be my companion in a unique way. And He shared every moment of that day.

The Lord and I had a hearty laugh at the 3-D movie, which showed alien, enthralling underwater critters seeming to come within a foot of my face.

I told Him, "You really *are* creative, Lord. You must have worked overtime on *those*." I could almost hear Him chuckle. We had quite a conversation there in the soft darkness. The movie was designed to give the feeling of swimming underwater, without all the paraphernalia, and I said to my companion, "Will I be able to do that in Heaven? Swim with the sea creatures with no fear, no air tank, not even getting *wet*?"

He said, "Even better than that!"

In 3-D illusion, we soared on a hang glider far above the land and water, and I asked, "This too?"

And He responded, "Even better."

I felt I could reach out and touch the soft necks of giraffes and nuzzle the plumes of the giant emu. "This too?" I queried, and He answered, "Better."

I left the movie to view the live shows, and the Lord and I laughed together as the porpoises spun and twisted and threw balls, splashing me, chattering with high squeaks. I felt as if God was grinning with me in delight as the seals clapped for themselves. He was beside me as we stared fascinated at the divers feeding the sharks, porpoises, and turtles. He was my companion as I enjoyed a hot dog on a stone table in the sun with seagulls staring at every mouthful, hoping for a handout.

We had a thoroughly delightful day, the Lord and I. On the way home, humming as I drove along the ocean, I said, "That was great! Thanks for being such a special companion to me today."

And the Lord answered my heart, "Carole, I'm your companion *every day*. But on many days, you aren't aware of My presence and you ignore Me as though I weren't with you. I long for you to be aware."

---

*Lord, I long to be aware! Even in my humdrum days — perhaps especially in my humdrum days — make me attuned to Your presence in the same way I am when I make it a point to seek You out.*

"Never will I leave you;
  never will I forsake you." (Hebrews 13:5)

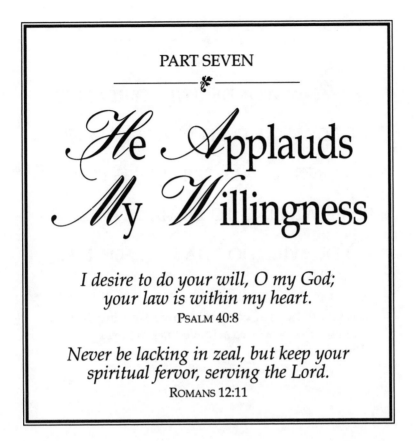

# PART SEVEN

# He Applauds My Willingness

*I desire to do your will, O my God;
your law is within my heart.*
PSALM 40:8

*Never be lacking in zeal, but keep your
spiritual fervor, serving the Lord.*
ROMANS 12:11

---------------- ❦ ----------------

# *H*OW WONDERFUL TO REALIZE,

## LORD, THAT EVEN WHEN I AM NOT

## WILLING . . . ALL IT TAKES IS FOR ME

## TO BE WILLING TO BE *MADE WILLING!*

## YOU WILL DO THAT . . . FOR ME!

It is God who is at work within you, giving you the
will and the power to achieve his purpose.
(Philippians 2:13, PH)

# THIRTY-FIVE

# *Because I Said*

*I*t was a simple story, but one that caught my heart.

She wanted to help, and so, because she was a nurse, she joined eighteen other medically trained people and journeyed to a poverty-stricken third-world country to help alleviate suffering by treating sick and injured people.

After working sixteen hours every day for two weeks, the clinic doors closed, and utterly exhausted, she headed toward the bus for home. Glancing up, she saw hundreds upon hundreds of sick and injured people waiting outside the clinic for treatment they would now never receive. She began to weep.

"Lord," she cried, "we haven't even made a *dent* in the need. What's the use? Have we done any good at all?"

As she turned to enter the bus, a hand tugged at her sleeve. There stood a man she scarcely recognized. Several days before his face had been distended and grotesque from a number of abscessed teeth, his feet so swollen with edema that he couldn't get on his shoes. They'd given him antibiotics, later pulled the abscessed teeth, and now he stood before her — smiling, pain free, with shoes on his feet. He smiled widely, thrust a small bouquet of flowers into her hand, and said simply, "Thank you for saving my life."

On the bus, she glanced out at the now-dark harbor as a single light came on. Then another. And another. Until the other side of the harbor was ablaze with light. God whispered to her heart, "This is how you helped — by treating My little ones — one person at a time."

---

Often in the ministry of marriage that God has given to Jack and me, I feel like we have tried to staunch the tide of eroding relationships — the pain, divorce, unhappiness in marriages — by putting a figurative finger into a small hole in a dike. But as I look up, I see water pouring through from a million other holes, and I cry, "Oh, what's the use?! Why are we doing this?"

And the Lord answers, "*Because I asked you to.*"

When Simon Peter had fished all night and caught nothing, the Lord, after teaching the people from Simon's boat, told him to go out into deep water and let down the nets for a catch.

Simon answered, "Master, we've worked hard all night and haven't caught anything. But because you say so, I will let down the nets." And they caught so many fish their nets began to break (Luke 5:4-6)!

*Because God says so.* This should be motivation enough for me to do what He asks.

I had to blink the other day as I read 1 Corinthians 4. The Apostle Paul discussed the matter of having a clear conscience before God and the fact that we mustn't judge anything, because God will bring to light what is hidden in darkness and will expose the motives of men's hearts. Then came this astonishing verse (5): "At that time each will receive. . . ."

Now wouldn't you think, based on the previous discussion, it would read "receive God's judgment"? But no. It says, "At that time each will receive his *praise* from God" (emphasis added).

I had to let that sink in slowly. Then I realized two things. Those who belong to Christ will never be judged for sins because Christ died for those sins. The sins are gone — buried in the depths of the deepest sea to be remembered no more by God! (He will judge our works, but that's a different matter entirely.)

The other thing I saw with astonishment is that God will praise *me*! Unbelievable! The God of the universe who deserves all *my* praise, will praise *me*!

*For what?* my thoughts asked. Well, I don't think it's going to be the "public stuff." No, I think it is going to be the secret decisions of obedience that no one sees except God and me. Those times I determined to give thanks instead of grumble. Making the choice to rejoice instead of feeling sorry for myself. The decisions I made to act loving when I wanted to erupt in anger. To hang in there when I felt like giving up . . . *just because He said.*

---

*Father, I confess that often in my life, "just because You said" isn't enough motivation for me. I want quick rewards, visible signs of blessing, and yes, I admit, often I want the applause of men.*

*Oh, Father! May I obey You often . . . in the secret places of my heart . . . and do it . . . just because You said!*

"Whoever has my commands and obeys them, he is the one who loves me. He who loves me will be loved by my Father, and I too will love him and show myself to him." (John 14:21)

THIRTY-SIX

# Beware of Dog

*J*ack came in chuckling. He had stopped at a traffic light directly behind a woman on a motorcycle who had a small Lhasa apso dog riding behind her in a custom-built carrier complete with wrap-around windscreen. A sign in large letters on the carrier said: "BEWARE OF DOG." And then in smaller letters underneath it said: "He's small, but he knows Kung Fu!"

I would like to meet that woman! Obviously, she has an attitude about life that is positive and upbeat, and she approaches life with a sense of humor.

At times, instead of feeling postive, I feel like positively screaming!

When I look into the Bible, I realize I'm not the only one who feels that way. Obviously, the psalmist who wrote Psalm 69 wasn't having a good day. He says, "Save me, O my God. The floods have risen. Deeper and deeper I sink in the mire; the waters rise around me. I have wept until I am exhausted; my throat is dry and hoarse; my eyes are swollen with weeping, waiting for my God to act. I cannot even count all those who hate me without cause . . . O God, you know so well how stupid I am, and you know all my sins" (TLB). As he goes on and on, I'm right there with him.

But as I look more closely, I'm aware of something else. His lament is the way he is *feeling*, but it isn't his *attitude*. His attitude is expressed in verse 16 as he says, "O Jehovah,

120

answer my prayers, for your lovingkindness is wonderful, your mercy is so plentiful, so tender and so kind" (TLB).

In one day, I have a variety of feelings. I can feel sad, discouraged, happy, frustrated, angry, elated, envious, desperate, thankful, grieving, ineffective, and anxious.

That's human. Nothing right or wrong about having feelings.

However, an attitude is a *mental position* concerning a situation or life itself. Feelings to me are like the temperature, while attitude is the climate of my life.

All through Scripture, I see both feelings and attitudes portrayed.

Second Corinthians 6:10 (TLB) says, "Our hearts ache [a feeling], but at the same time we have the joy of the Lord [an attitude]." And Psalm 42:5-6 states, "Why are you downcast, O my soul? Why so disturbed within me? [Those are feelings.] Put your hope in God, for I will yet praise him, my Savior and my God. [That's a predetermined attitude.]"

Feelings flood and I cannot stop that flood; attitudes are chosen and are something I *put into practice* every day.

The Lord Jesus Himself talked about that. He said that we are all like His mother and brothers if we hear God's Word and put it into practice (Luke 8:21).

I know. It plays a lot harder than it records.

How do I "hear" the Word? By listening to messages about it. By reading it carefully. By studying it, memorizing it, and meditating on it. I am to "consider carefully how I listen" (Luke 8:18). I need to examine my heart closely to see if I really am dwelling in His Word *richly* (Colossians 3:16), or am I paddling around in the shallows instead of going for the depths?

How do I retain it? I'll retain it if I meditate on it, if I *learn it by heart*, if I dig deep and then dwell even deeper.

And how do I persevere? *With all my might*. As though my life depended on it. With the knowledge that not to do so is sin.

Colossians 3 convicts me every time I read it—especially the part that says I am to "rid myself" of all the uglies in my life, such as rage, malice, slander, lying, or greed. And then

I am to clothe myself in all the beautiful things God wants to see in me, such as compassion, kindness, humility, gentleness, and patience. God has given me His Holy Spirit to enable me to be able to do this but the *choice* is mine . . . my will is involved. To have the kinds of attitudes that God wants to see in my life will take the rest of my life, and I must persevere.

I am reminded of a man who came up to a violinist who had just given a brilliant performance and said, "I'd give my life to be able to play like that."

The violinist looked the man straight in the eye and said, "I have."

It will take the rest of my life to be clothed with attitudes of godliness. For sure, I am a person in process.

But, friends, we'll never do it unless we *begin*.

*Father God, help me not to be discouraged with my feelings but instead to determine to choose godly attitudes. May I hear Your Word with my heart, retain it with my soul, and persevere in obeying You . . . starting now and continuing for the rest of my life.*

As God's chosen people, holy and dearly loved, clothe yourselves with compassion, kindness, humility, gentleness and patience. Bear with each other and forgive whatever grievances you may have against one another. Forgive as the Lord forgave you. And over all these virtues put on love, which binds them all together in perfect unity. Let the peace of Christ rule in your hearts, since as members of one body you were called to peace. And be thankful. (Colossians 3:12-15)

# THIRTY-SEVEN

# The Sheep

---

*T*he fire glowed warm on that cold pre-Christmas evening as I snuggled down on the couch to savor the day's mail. Sometimes, among all the newsletters and cards, like the first bright star, a personal letter shines against the dark sky of life.

This was such a one. It began by quoting a recent newspaper article titled: "Snow Bunny Turns Out to Be a Sheep." Seems the ski patrol at Telluride found a ewe on a closed ski run where they were setting off avalanche charges. Poor thing had somehow been left behind when the flock was rounded up in September. The sheep apparently had been living on grass foraged from beneath more than five feet of snow.

The men, riding a snowmobile, roped the stubborn, less-than-cooperative ewe and pulled her to patrol headquarters. That night the ewe feasted on spinach salad, potatoes, and carrots. The next day, she was loaded onto a toboggan and transported down the slope amid the skiers and finally reunited with the flock.

My friend continued, "What a delightful picture I have in my mind of that sheep sitting atop the toboggan with ears flapping behind, people gawking, as she sped down the mountain—her eyes as big as saucers! I could not help being stricken with this funny little story because of the parallels I can draw from it to my own life this year. You see, I've been that silly sheep up on the mountain foraging for what I could — trying to survive in a winter place on what I dug up — thinking I'm getting along and taking care of myself okay — but without enough sense to open my eyes and really see the winter around me . . . I, like that sheep, tend to balk and fight back — too ignorant to realize that I could be feasting on 'spinach, carrots, and potatoes' instead of nibbling frozen bits of grass."

The point she emphasizes is one I sometimes need: I tend to cling to the comfortable and familiar, even when the grass is about gone and the Shepherd wants me elsewhere. I'm terrified of the rope, not realizing it is a rope of love. Scared of the toboggan ride to unknown destinations. Wide-eyed and fearful of the unexplored and untested.

So I balk. And sometimes God has to prod and push to get me to the place He has for me.

He opens a door, and I say, "Hey, I like it where I am."

He calls, and I say, "Let's do that later."

Sad that I do that. For as my friend said, "I guess I'll start feasting again and maybe even go for a toboggan ride down the mountain. I'd love to have you come too!"

*Yes. Me too.*

———◆———

*Father God, I really don't want to lag behind You — or run ahead of You, either. Thank You for the times You've made me uncomfortable, for pushing and prodding me even when I don't like it. Help me to stop paddling in the comfortable shallows and swim out into the depths of Your wonders for me.*

"I know the plans that I have for you," declares the LORD, "plans for welfare and not for calamity to give you a future and a hope." (Jeremiah 29:11, NASB)

# THIRTY-EIGHT

# Seeing Through
# a Glass Darkly

*J*anuary 14, 1986. Ghana, West Africa.

I sighed as I tried to find a more comfortable position in the straight-backed chair. My notebook lay opened in my lap, and I read over what I had written . . .

---

Jack is very ill. He is lying in the double bed in this blue box room with the slanted white ceiling. Every few minutes, he opens his eyes, but his look is glazed, unfocused. After he manages to swallow a few spoonfuls of soup, he falls weakly back onto the pillow in utter exhaustion.

Friends serve us unselfishly, fixing meals, taking him to the hospital. Doctors are baffled by his sickness.

In two days we are supposed to fly to Nigeria, but the prospect of that is slim. Telephone and communication lines are broken between Ghana and Nigeria, and we are concerned. How can we get word to friends in Nigeria who have planned seminars and meetings for us and who will be at the plane to meet us?

I just read: "Hear my cry, O God; listen to my prayer. From the ends of the earth I call to you [that's how far away I feel I am!], I call as my heart grows faint; lead me to the rock that is higher than I" (Psalm 61:1-2).

And I pray, "Lord, my heart is growing faint. It seems

the more I walk with You, the less You explain Yourself to me. Perhaps it's because You know You don't have to! My heart *will* trust even for this trip. People have given money to make this journey possible. We felt You leading. Ministry to married couples here is critical, and we came eager to be Your vessels for help and healing.

"Then, right in the middle of this trip, Jack collapsed so that we can't go on. I am very confused!

"But this time, Father, I ask not why. This time I ask *what*. What is it You want us to learn about You? Please make it so clear we can't miss it.

"Right now, I'm numb—as though in shock. My mind is reeling. Please clarify, punctuate, and then seal in Your lesson. I'm waiting."

---

The hot, humid air pressed in on me. I put down my pen and rubbed my neck gently, trying to get out the kink, but it didn't work. I wondered what the next few days would hold.

What we feared, happened. Friends tried every way to contact those in Nigeria that we weren't coming—but the telephones weren't working; telegraph lines were down; even the American Embassy couldn't get through. Finally, friends in London were contacted with the hope that they could make connections to Nigeria, but that too was unsuccessful. Our Nigerian friends drove many hours to meet a plane we weren't on; only then did they call our mutual contact in London to find out why we weren't on that plane. (Somehow the phones worked from Nigeria to London, but not from London—or anyplace else—to call them!) It was too late to postpone the conference, so people came from all over Nigeria to find that the speakers hadn't shown up!

A few days later Jack, white and weak, managed to board a plane for home. We were both discouraged, frustrated, and terribly weary.

One year later God allowed us to go to Nigeria, and for many, it was a *better* time. Friends who had filled in at the last minute to speak for the previous year's conference experienced unusual grace, and people were helped greatly. Once again, God had shown us that He does *all things well* . . . even when *we* don't understand!

Someday when I get to Heaven, I'm going to ask the Lord why He allowed all those irritating, frustrating, and discouraging events to happen to so many people. And when He tells me, I am sure that I will stand in awe and wonder at His incredible plan!

But for now? Someone said, "Much of life falls between the cracks." Another mused, "Much of the Christian life is just hanging on."

Courage doesn't demand understanding. But the Lord has assured over and over, "Be strong and courageous. Do not be afraid or terrified . . . for the LORD your God goes with you; he will never leave you nor forsake you" (Deuteronomy 31:6).

Really . . . isn't that enough?

---

*Dear Father, I forget sometimes that You are in my moments. I remember that You are in my weeks, and months, and years. But I forget You are also in my moments.*

*So when a seeming mistake, a change of schedule, a cancellation of an event occurs, I tend to think of it as a delay, an unvalued hour or day, a parenthesis in the God-planned time of my life.*

*Yet those delays, cancellations, changes, have been scheduled into my life by You. Help me to remember that.*

*Thank You that You are in my moments. All of them.*

But I trust in you, O LORD;
    I say, "You are my God."
My times are in your hands;
        deliver me from my enemies and from those who
            pursue me.
Let your face shine on your servant;
        save me in your unfailing love. (Psalm 31:14-16)

# THIRTY-NINE

# The Marks of a Servant

———◆———

*T*he young man leaned forward intently and asked, "*How* can you know if you have the heart of a servant?" It was not a casual question.

His older companion paused a moment and answered simply, "By your response when you are treated like one."

Recently I've had the opportunity to observe my own response when it seemed nothing, and no one, had "served me"—from the airlines to the weather to people in general. I'm sure I flunked the course in "Servant Attitude 101."

Let me explain.

I've always felt things ought to go right on your birthday (don't you?). Last Saturday mine began well as we boarded our flight to St. Louis, which connected to a flight to Atlanta scheduled to arrive at 4:00 p.m. There we planned to rent a car and drive to Chattanooga for the start of a conference the next morning, stopping to have a leisurely birthday dinner along the way.

When we arrived at the departure gate in St. Louis, however, a delay was announced over the loudspeaker—"further word in thirty minutes, don't leave the gate area." The same announcement was repeated thirty minutes later . . . and thirty minutes later . . . and thirty minutes later. Finally, the airlines decided that the plane's generator would have to be replaced, and we were put on another aircraft for the hour flight to Atlanta. But thunderstorms in the Atlanta area caused us to circle until fuel was low, so we landed at Nashville for refueling. The plane's air conditioning had ceased by this time so it was hot. No ice. No soft drinks. Everyone miserable. The plane sat on the ground a couple of hours, then took off again, circled the Atlanta airport and *finally* landed at 9:30 p.m.

We proceeded to the baggage claim area where, after more holdups, we discovered that no baggage had been transferred from the disabled plane in St. Louis. The next plane (the original one, fixed by that time) would be in at 11:10 p.m. It seemed our only choice was to wait.

Hungry and weary, we walked to the only place open that time of night—a crowded pay-before-you-eat coffee shop—to have a bite of supper. Our food grew cold as Jack stood in a long line to pay. I watched, dismayed, and thought, *So much for my birthday dinner!*

Finally at 11:45 p.m. the luggage arrived. We got a rental car and headed out, intending to get a motel just outside of Atlanta and drive on to Chattanooga in the morning. But "no vacancy" signs were all we spotted until, one-and-a-half-hours' drive from Atlanta, we found a room and crawled into bed at 2:00 a.m. for a short four hours of sleep. At the conference site, we had time only to hastily stuff our things in the room before beginning to speak at 10:15 a.m.

Walking up four flights of stairs to our tiny, unairconditioned room, we found no sheets with which to make up the beds or towels to use in the bath down the hall. No one was assigned to act as host or clued us in on the activities, prayer groups, or procedure for meals. Days passed before anyone even invited us to sit with their family for a meal and not a single person asked us—the "outsiders"—to sightsee or participate in planned activities.

I thought things would surely get better! They didn't! It was a strange conference. During the whole week we continued to feel as if we were outside looking in on a very clannish group of people.

Our impression was that the conference was mostly for vacation with a little bit of spiritual and practical input—different from what was said when we were invited to speak.

No one expected it to be one where God does a deep work in hearts—and so of course, He didn't. For us, the time was disappointing in every way, and I felt, well, put out.

But then I remembered the statement concerning the heart of a servant—that it was demonstrated by a person's response when treated like one. I was aware that in many ways we had been treated as servants that week. The airlines hadn't served us well, the weather had made schedules unbearable, and the people at the conference weren't ministering to us, either.

*Just like a servant.*

I grinned ruefully to myself and talked to the Lord.

---

*Lord, that is just what I am, isn't it? Your servant. Thanks for the reminder—I need it often! Forgive me for forgetting, for expecting more, for thinking I should be treated differently—better. Your Son served, and He is my example. Help me to desire to minister unto rather than feeling like I should be ministered to.*

"Just as the Son of Man did not come to be served, but to serve, and to give his life as a ransom for many." (Matthew 20:28)

# FORTY

# *Mind-Boggling*

We sat side by side — Jack and I — and eagerly opened the sturdy square box, which had arrived that morning containing the new lap-top computer he had given me for Christmas. We carefully laid out all the program disks, battery packs, adaptors. At last, we opened the thick book explaining how to use it.

It took me three horrific months to learn my first computer and word-processing program, which is now, I'm sure, listed among the antiques in computer catalogs. (I can't even *give* the thing away!)

As I read and reread and re-reread the first chapter of the manual, I felt again as if I had moved to a foreign country before taking a language course. Nothing made sense.

Sometimes that's how I feel reading another manual — the one about life and death — called the Bible.

This morning I read in Colossians 2:9-12 that I have been given *fullness* in Christ, that I've been "buried with him in baptism and raised with him through your faith." I told myself, "That is too wonderful, too mind-boggling, too awesome, too big . . . for me even to begin to understand. But I believe it! I don't understand God's incredible love, goodness, or greatness. Sometimes I don't understand His seeming harshness either.

"It's like — another language, another culture, another perspective entirely."

131

I refocused on the computer manual and sighed. It was going to take a lot of study and I felt—well, *dumb.*

I have to realize someone with vast knowledge—which I don't have—wrote it.

It will take time to absorb and understand. Reading it over and over. Going through the steps one at a time. Making mistakes and starting over. Asking questions of people who know more than I do. Trying again. Knowing full well I'll never learn all it can do. Being content with using a fraction of its capabilities.

But this I know. . . . It works.

I will learn.

And I'm not talking just about computers.

---

*Father, You are so big! Thank You that though I am finite and You are infinite, though I am ignorant and You are wisdom, though I am lacking in knowledge and You have all knowledge, You have nevertheless promised to teach me what I need to know and to give me the wisdom I need.*

Such knowledge is too wonderful for me,
too lofty for me to attain. (Psalm 139:6)

Oh, the depth of the riches of the wisdom
and knowledge of God!
How unsearchable his judgments,
and his paths beyond tracing out! (Romans 11:33)

FORTY-ONE

# *Have I Accomplished Anything Today?*

The petite woman sat on my couch, brushed a hand over her silver hair, and sighed wearily. Concern lines shadowed her face—anxiety for an adult son who has multiple sclerosis, but who fiercely maintains his independence by keeping his own apartment. Patiently, she and her husband journey over to their son's home several times a day—early and late morning, lunch, afternoon, bedtime. They care for him. Serve him. Get his meals. Feed him. Bathe him.

She said to me, "You know, yesterday I was so tired I didn't feel like doing anything. So I didn't make any calls on customers. I just went home."

"Did you take a nap?" I asked, knowing she needed one.

"No." She paused and then said triumphantly, "I got caught up on the *ironing*."

I smiled, knowing how she felt. The sight of freshly ironed clothes made her feel she had *done* something. It gave her a sense of accomplishment. I can identify with that.

Fortunately, God has a different perspective!

I remember a day not so long ago. I'd gone as fast as I could go, making meals, cleaning, taking care of little bodies, going on errands in order to make more meals and entertain the little bodies. At the end of the day I thought, *Wow, I sure haven't accomplished much today!*

Then God reminded me gently, "Carole, what is your purpose on earth?"

"To serve You, Lord, and to serve Your people."

"What have you *been* doing?"

I thought a moment and with new insight responded, "Why, I've been serving You, Lord, as I serve Your people! The people may be small ones today — well, yes, my husband isn't so small, and I've been serving him today, too. But I've been doing things all day for Your people."

"So what have you accomplished?" He asked my heart.

"I've done Your will today," I whispered.

I felt His smile. "That's all I ask, dear child."

*Father, it's so easy when I'm meeting needs that seem trivial to forget how important each one of Your children is to You. Thank You for the gentle ways You remind me of what is truly significant.*

"Whoever wants to become great among you must be your servant, and whoever wants to be first must be slave of all. For even the Son of Man did not come to be served, but to serve, and to give his life as a ransom for many." (Mark 10:43-45)

Whatever you do, work at it with all your heart, as working for the Lord, not for men, since you know that you will receive an inheritance from the Lord as a reward. It is the Lord Christ you are serving. (Colossians 3:23-24)

# FORTY-TWO

# *My Face Is Red!*

—————◄►•◄►—————

"Oh, my goodness. I'm so *embarrassed!*" The plumpish woman hung her head and with a faint wail in her voice said, "I didn't realize you were the *speaker!*"

As the women were gathering for the conference, she and I had chatted for twenty minutes over coffee. *We'd a nice conversation*, I thought. But now, after the meeting, she acted humiliated and was apologizing profusely. Why?

I wanted to ask, "What would you have done differently if you had known?" Instead, I gave her a little hug and told her there was no reason for her to have recognized me or even to have glanced at my name tag to make a connection. She, at least, had been friendly, had reached out to a person she didn't know. I am always grateful for that.

I remembered a time when I sat down in the front row next to a couple of young women who glanced at me, looked away, and went on with their conversation. I longed to have them briefly introduce themselves to a stranger. Not because I was the speaker, which they couldn't have known, but because I was obviously alone. Because I was and am a fellow traveler in a rather hostile world. Because I longed for a smile, a welcome, a handshake. Because I am "everywoman," and there were, no doubt, a number of us at the conference.

I glanced at my embarrassed new friend and reflected again. Being the speaker or singer or performer shouldn't put a person in a special category of relating. Every time I read James 2:1, I get a twinge. It says, "My brothers, as believers in our glorious Lord Jesus Christ, don't show favoritism." That's pretty clear. Some synonyms for the word *favoritism* are bias, predisposed, prejudice, and discrimination.

Showing partiality to anyone at all is forbidden by God!

Right in the middle of a whole lot of commands in Leviticus 19, God speaks to this particular issue: "Do not pervert justice; do not show partiality to the poor or favoritism to the great, but judge your neighbor fairly" (verse 15).

Two huge "things not to do" — partiality to the poor and favoritism to the great.

We Christians do go to extremes! We seem to be either celebrity-conscious or down-and-outer conscious . . . or both. Do you know someone with a tender heart who will get up from a church pew and plow through a crowd of people in order to greet an obviously needy stranger, but who wouldn't turn around to greet a well-dressed Mr. and Mrs. Average newcomer? That's reverse partiality.

But most of us err on the other side of favoritism. We are inclined to treat those of intellect or wealth or position in a slightly more differential way than we treat the "everywoman" stranger among us. We smile warmly and extend cordiality to elevated special folk and often ignore the seeming nonperson among us. The beautifully dressed are greeted politely, but we are a bit uncomfortable with the poorly dressed who walk through the door of our church.

Somehow, those with a cultured English accent are accepted with alacrity, while those who murder the Kings English are shunned.

We listen intently to the person with a "doctor" in front of her name but are impatient when the illiterate or uneducated speak.

And wealth impresses! Let me tell you how I know.

Jack and I came out of a restaurant in San Diego to see a white stretch limousine parked in front, a bored driver looking out the window. Jokingly Jack asked, "How about a ride to our hotel?" After stammering a moment, the driver suddenly smiled and said, "Hop in."

It was our turn to stammer. But the chauffeur said he

really needed the experience (it was only his second time driving!), and we ended up having a short tour of San Diego at night.

As we drove to our hotel, Tim (the chauffeur whom we'd gotten to know by this time) said, "Now don't get out. I need the practice opening the doors for customers."

I laughed and said, "You'll never get the chance!"

Sure enough. The two hotel doormen had a race to see who got to the door of the limousine first! We certainly hadn't had that treatment previously when we drove up with our own road-dirty, older-model car.

It was a graphic example of preferential treatment. Treatment that can be smiled at when a doorman does it. But treatment that, according to the Bible, God *hates*.

---

*Lord, keep me from treating one member of the Body of Christ differently from another. I want to give honor to those You specifically tell me to honor—the aged, the elders—but also to honor, respect, and prize all my family in Christ. May I reach out to strangers as friends. Remind me to visit with a speaker or artist in the same way I would an attendee— and an attendee in the very same way I would a speaker.*

*Make me sensitive to Your command, "Brothers, don't show favoritism."*

*May it be so!*

Now that you have purified yourselves by obeying the truth so that you have sincere love for your brothers, love one another deeply, from the heart. For you have been born again, not of perishable seed, but of imperishable, through the living and enduring word of God. (1 Peter 1:22-23)

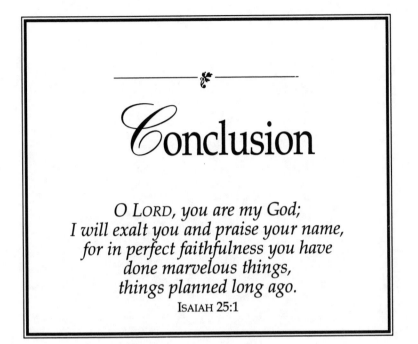

# Conclusion

*O L*ORD*, you are my God;*
*I will exalt you and praise your name,*
*for in perfect faithfulness you have*
*done marvelous things,*
*things planned long ago.*
I*SAIAH* 25:1

# FORTY-THREE

# I Don't Deserve Spring

he sun splashed warm on our faces as we munched lunch—Jack a hamburger and me a pita-pocket stuffed with chicken salad. We gazed at the view before us and sighed with contentment. On this newly made May day, a snow-mantled Pikes Peak jutted into the deep-blue Colorado sky, framed by the unusual red rocks of the Garden of the Gods park. Jack grinned at me and said, "I don't deserve this!"

And I responded, "Nor I."

The next day I walked around Serendipity Circle (believe it or not, our street is called Serendipity—a serendipity in itself) and drank in the smell of lilacs, the flowering trees, the edge-of-the-mountain freshness on a perfect, pure day. Mentally, I raised my arms to encompass all that was around me and whispered, "Quite frankly, I don't deserve *spring*!"

It's true. If I got what I deserved, it would always be the barest, most dismal, darkest, coldest winter.

Then I lifted my heart to Heaven and said, "Father, thank You. Thank You that You don't give me what I deserve. But instead, because of Your grace and mercy, You give me beauty, and forgiveness, and love, and strength, and hope and . . . You give me *spring*."

Spring is just one more way God whispers love.

And I say, "Hallelujah!"

*Father, You've whispered Your love in my moments, in my days, and throughout the years. You've shown Yourself to me in the dailies of my life and in the momentous events. You've demonstrated Your wonder through my hopeless, empty, fruitless intervals, and in the times I've been filled with thanksgiving and praise.*

*You are continually whispering love to me.*

*Oh, Father, in future moments . . . in coming days . . . during the years I have left on earth . . . help me to hear You!*

The LORD said, "Go out and stand on the mountain in the presence of the LORD, for the LORD is about to pass by."

Then a great and powerful wind tore the mountains apart and shattered the rocks before the LORD, but the LORD was not in the wind. After the wind there was an earthquake, but the LORD was not in the earthquake. After the earthquake came a fire, but the LORD was not in the fire. And after the fire came a gentle whisper. (1 Kings 19:11-12)

He does not treat us as our sins deserve
    or repay us according to our iniquities.
For as high as the heavens are above the earth,
    so great is his love for those who fear him.
        (Psalm 103:10-11)

# *Author*

Carole Mayhall and her husband, Jack, have been with The Navigators since 1956. Currently, they are ministering in the department of Marriage and the Family. They travel extensively in the United States and overseas, speaking to individuals and groups concerning marriage and discipleship.

Carole has a ministry with women nationwide. She is the author of several books, including *Lord of My Rocking Boat* and *Words that Hurt, Words that Heal*. She and Jack co-authored *Marriage Takes More Than Love*.